D1595631

# The Mystery of Faith
## A Christian Creed for Today

*William V. Dych, S.J.*

A Michael Glazier Book
THE LITURGICAL PRESS
Collegeville, Minnesota

A Michael Glazier Book published by The Liturgical Press

Cover design by Fred Petters. Photo by Robin Pierzina, O.S.B.

| 1 | 2 | 3 | 4 | 5 | 6 | 7 | 8 |
|---|---|---|---|---|---|---|---|

**Library of Congress Cataloging-in-Publication Data**

Dych, William V.
   The mystery of faith : a Christian creed for today / William V. Dych.
     p.   cm.
   Includes bibliographical references.
   ISBN 0-8146-5514-9
   1. Lord's Supper—Catholic Church.  2. Spiritual life—Catholic Church.  3. Faith.  4. Catholic Church—Doctrines.  I. Title.
BX2215.2.D93  1995
230'.2—dc20                          94-3740
                                         CIP

# Contents

Κηρύασσω — Μκ 1.45  Λκ 4:18,19 , 1 Cor 9:27

ἐπικηρύσσω

ἀγγέλλω



Κήρυγμα , τος , τό

what is cried by a herald

1 Cor 1:21

# Introduction

In his study of the origins and historical development of the
Eucharistic liturgy, Josef Jungmann makes a series of observations
on the phrase *mysterium fidei,* or "the mystery of faith," in its liturgical usage. It occurs in the Roman rite as part of the memorial
of the Lord's words and actions with bread and wine at the Last
Supper. These latter are recorded with incidental variations by the
three Synoptic Gospels (Matt 26:26-29, Mark 14:22-25, Luke
22:17-20), and by Paul (1 Cor 11:23-26). Though the phrase itself is an addition to the New Testament accounts and its precise
origin is unknown, Jungmann finds it to be in widespread use at
least by the seventh century.[1]

Its position in the present liturgy immediately after the memorial
is itself significant in that it points to and proclaims the import of
the words and actions just completed: here is or this is the mystery
of our faith. Jungmann comments, first, that mystery here does
not refer "to the obscurity of what is here hidden from the senses,"
nor is it meant in the intellectual sense of something beyond understanding. Its meaning is rather quite concrete: mystery of faith
means a sacrament or symbol of faith. Faith in this context, then,
does not refer to the subjective act of believing, but to the objective faith of the Church. Moreover, continues Jungmann, this reality is not *a* mystery of faith, but *the* mystery of faith wherein "the
entire (objective) faith, the whole divine order of salvation is com-

[1] Josef Jungmann, *The Mass of the Roman Rite: Its Origins and Development*
(New York: Benziger, 1955) vol. 2, 199–201.

prised." The Lord's words and actions at the Last Supper solemnly commemorated in the liturgy represent a summary and recapitulation of Christian faith in its unity and entirety.[2]

Over the centuries this single mystery of Christian faith has been articulated into a large number of "mysteries," and these comments of Jungmann can help us not to lose sight of the forest for the trees. This liturgical text is an authentic piece of early Christian tradition in the sense that here the Church is proclaiming and handing on its understanding and interpretation of the scriptural narrative about Jesus. If in this sense authentic tradition points beyond itself to Scripture, Scripture too points beyond itself to the events it is narrating. As James Barr expresses it:

> Christian faith is not a set of ideas or a pattern of imagery; it may include these but they are not its essence. The essence is a set of historical facts—with, we must add, an interpretation of them in faith. The faith is based on some things which have taken place in history. . . .[3]

The liturgical actions and words represent such an interpretation of historical facts. They point back to the events narrated in Scripture as embodying and recapitulating the early Christian community's faith in Jesus and they proclaim "the mystery of faith" anew in commemorative words and actions.

Such a text would have fulfilled in its own day, and perhaps can also fulfill in our day, the requirements for what Karl Rahner calls "a short formula of Christian faith."[4] Such a formula is not a reduction or an attenuation or a watering down of Christian faith, but rather an abbreviation and summary of it. It is an attempt to express in brief and concise fashion the heart and core of Christian faith from out of which its manifold articulations have arisen over many centuries of doctrinal development. The purpose of such a short formula is to give people today an insight into the central mystery of Christian faith so that they can assimilate it and live it.

It is in Rahner's sense of a short formula that Jungmann says that the liturgical phrase *mysterium fidei* refers not to *a* mystery of faith, but to *the* mystery of faith. It refers to the central mystery

---

[2]*op. cit.,* 200–201.

[3]James Barr, *The Bible in the Modern World* (London: SCM Press, 1973) 76.

[4]See "The Need for a 'Short Formula' of Christian Faith" *Theological Investigations 9* (London and New York, 1972) 117–126.

which embodies the whole of Christian faith. This particular short formula has the advantage of being not just words or propositions, but actions as well. The words and actions together constitute the concrete symbol, the mystery of faith. Moreover, if these words and actions can be traced back to Jesus himself, a question we shall examine in the first chapter, then this particular symbol of faith in Jesus would reflect something of his own self-understanding.

The following chapters will attempt to show why these liturgical words and actions do, indeed, represent *the* mystery or symbol of faith in Jungmann's sense and thereby provide for Christians today a short formula of faith in the sense in which Rahner uses this phrase. They shall ask basically two questions. The first is a question about Jesus, the Christological question first posed by Jesus himself in the New Testament: "Who do you say that I am?" The second is a question about faith: What does it mean to believe in him? Both questions are perennial questions for the Church in its ongoing effort to live and hand on the mystery of faith.

# 1

# Origins

There seems to be little doubt that the scriptural narrative about the Last Supper and the liturgical commemoration of the event it narrates actually put us in touch with the historical Jesus of Nazareth.[1] We are presuming here, however, that the New Testament Gospels are not history books nor do they give us a biography of Jesus. They are books of faith which express the early Christian communities' faith in Jesus in a great variety of ways. Nevertheless, this faith has its roots in history, in a real historical person and in real historical events.[2] The Last Supper narratives, though written from out of the faith of the early Christian communities, do give us a glimpse of the historical Jesus of Nazareth in whom they placed their faith.

It is important, then, to distinguish in the gospel material between a historical report of Jesus of Nazareth and faith statements made about him, for example, that Jesus is the Christ. This distinction precludes reading the Gospels in a fundamentalist way as straightforward historical records. The distinction, however, must

[1] This is the conclusion reached by John P. Meier in his article "Jesus" in *The New Jerome Biblical Commentary,* eds. R. E. Brown, J. A. Fitzmyer, R. E. Murphy (London: Geoffrey Chapman, and Englewood Cliffs, N. J.: Prentice Hall, 1989) 1327 (hereafter *NJBC*). He bases his conclusion on the presence of the supper narrative, including Jesus' words and actions with the bread and wine, in so many different New Testament traditions. See also J. Jeremias, *The Eucharistic Words of Jesus* (London: SCM Press, 1966) 101, 201–203 (hereafter *Eucharistic Words*).

[2] See the comments of James Barr on this point in the Introduction, 6.

not be allowed to become a total separation, as though what Christians said in faith about Jesus had nothing to do with who he actually was or what he actually said and did. Such historical skepticism like its opposite, fundamentalism, reduces Jesus to a mythological figure and Christian faith to an ahistorical idealism. Rather it was the real historical person and the real historical events which evoked the faith response of the first Christians.

Like all the material in the Gospels, the Last Supper narratives were told and handed on by word of mouth for several decades before they were written down. In the case of the Eucharistic words and actions of Jesus, the setting for this handing on was the Church's early liturgy. The words and actions of Jesus were repeated in ritual form as he had directed: "Do this in memory of me" (1 Cor 11:24, 25; Luke 22:19). In addition to being part of the scriptural narratives, then, these words and actions were also an independent tradition as part of the early liturgy. This fact is important for several reasons. First, it explains the differences in the New Testament accounts, for the different versions reflect the different ritual form the words and actions had taken in the widely scattered communities where the ritual was performed. Rather than the liturgy's being based on the New Testament texts, these are based on and reflect the earlier practice of the first Christian communities.

Second, this situation attests to the very early nature of the Last Supper material. According to the analysis of Joachim Jeremias,[3] the oldest written form of the Eucharistic tradition, that in 1 Corinthians 11:23-25, was probably written in 54 A.D. The text reads:

> The Lord Jesus on the night when he was delivered up took bread, and having given thanks, broke it and said: "This is my body which is for you. Do this in memory of me." In the same way after supper also the cup saying: "This cup is the new covenant in my blood. Do this as often as you drink it in memory of me."

Paul introduces this passage by saying that he has already delivered this tradition to the community at Corinth orally, that is, at the beginning of his missionary work there in 49 A.D. Paul says further that what he delivered to them he had received himself, so that the tradition antedates his work in Corinth. This places the

---

[3] See *Eucharistic Words,* 186–189.

tradition at least as early as sometime in the middle of the 40s. Moreover, Paul says that it is "from the Lord" that he has received it, indicating that he sees the tradition as having its origin in Jesus himself.

Behind Paul's Greek version, of course, lies the original semitic tradition that would have been the language used by the earliest Jewish Christian communities in their liturgy. For a variety of linguistic reasons, mainly the number of semitisms in the Markan version (Mark 14:22-24), it is most likely that Mark's account most truly reflects linguistically the original semitic tradition that lies behind the Greek tradition in Paul.[4] Mark's version reads as follows:

> And as they were eating, he took bread, and having said the blessing, he broke it and gave it to them and said: "Take, this is my body." And taking the cup, having given thanks, he gave it to them and they all drank it, and he said to them: "This is my blood of the covenant which is poured out for many."

It cannot be concluded, however, that Mark preserves the original form of the tradition intact. For Mark's text, too, shows signs of development and adaption to liturgical usage, for example, in drawing together the words over the bread and wine which were originally separated by the intervening meal. Both Paul and Luke give evidence of this in the phrase "after supper" which introduces Jesus's words and actions with the wine.[5] Jeremias does conclude, however, that the semitic tradition which Mark most truly reflects belongs "to the first decade after the death of Jesus."[6]

Mark's version also throws light on another important question: whether behind the liturgical texts preserved in Paul and the Gospels there is discernible a still earlier level of historical narrative. In other words, what stands at the beginning of the Last Supper tradition, liturgy or historical report? In the fact that Mark begins the pericope with "and," and then repeats it five times in the course of the text (see above), Jeremias sees "a certain indication of the semitic historical report."[7] For this is an established characteristic of Palestinian historical writing as is evident in the Old Testament historical books. Luke also has "and" at the be-

[4]*Eucharistic Words,* 188–189.
[5]See R. J. Karris, "The Gospel According to Luke," *NJBC,* 715.
[6]*Eucharistic Words,* 189.
[7]Ibid., 192. See also 174.

ginning of his report (Luke 22:19). See above, on the other hand, the more solemn beginning of Paul, "The Lord Jesus on the night when he was betrayed," an indication of the liturgical stylizing of the original narrative. Jeremias concludes that "at the beginning there stands not liturgy, but historical account."[8]

Since the early semitic tradition can be traced back to the first decade after the death of Jesus, he considers the opposite hypothesis completely improbable. This would maintain that at such an early stage the Christian communities freely created their liturgical celebration of the Lord's Supper and then freely fabricated the New Testament accounts of the Last Supper as an aetiological legend to support their practice. The evidence points to the opposite conclusion, namely, that the Church's liturgical practice is based on a preliturgical narrative tradition which itself points to the historical Jesus. We are justified, then, in concluding that:

> . . . the common core of the tradition of the account of the Lord's Supper—what Jesus said at the Last Supper—is preserved to us in an essentially reliable form.[9]

If, indeed, we can speak with confidence of what Jesus said and did at the Last Supper, we must now ask what he meant by his words and actions.

The background against which these words and actions must be understood is the Jewish Passover celebration. Whether or not the Last Supper was a Passover meal is a disputed question. The chronology of the Synoptic Gospels seems to indicate that it was. See, for example, Luke's references to the preparations for the "Passover supper" and to Jesus' desire to "eat this Passover" with his disciples before he died (Luke 22:8-15). The Gospel of John, on the other hand, seems to situate the meal on the eve of Passover. It says, for example, that the Jewish accusers of Jesus "did not enter the praetorium, so that they might not be defiled, but might eat the Passover" (John 18:28), placing the trial and crucifixion of Jesus before the Passover feast. Whichever may have been the case, there is no doubt that the Passover in Jerusalem was the historical context within which the final events in the life of Jesus, including the Last Supper, took place.

[8]Ibid.

[9]*Eucharistic Words*, 203. See also Meier's concurring judgment in "Jesus," *NJBC*, 1327.

The meaning and the sequence of events at the Passover supper, then, can throw light on Jesus' own words and actions at his final meal with his disciples.[10] The meal began with a preliminary course which included the blessing and drinking of the first of several cups of wine. This explains Luke's reference to a cup of wine blessed by Jesus and shared by the disciples at the very beginning of the meal (Luke 22:17). Then followed the Passover liturgy which included a meditation on the original Exodus event being commemorated and an interpretation of the connection of various aspects of the meal with the original event. For example, the unleavened bread was a reminder of the misery their people had endured in Egypt, the bitter herbs represented their state of slavery, and the Passover lamb recalled God's mercy in passing over their households. The liturgy ended with the drinking of the second cup of wine. After the liturgy came the main meal which included the Passover lamb, unleavened bread, and bitter herbs.

But before the main meal the head of the household spoke a blessing over the unleavened bread, and at the end of the meal he spoke a blessing over the third cup of wine. This is important because they are the most likely places for the words and actions of Jesus over the bread and wine. According to the Passover rubrics, the head of the household sat up from his reclining position, took a cake of unleavened bread, and recited a blessing over it in the name of all. After the "Amen" of his table companions, he broke the bread and distributed a piece to each of them. These rubrics have a clear echo in the New Testament accounts that Jesus "took bread," and, "having said the blessing" or "having given thanks," "he broke it and gave it to them." It is at this point that the words of Jesus are introduced with the phrase, "and said," so that it would seem the words of Jesus were spoken during the distribution of the bread which normally took place in silence. They were an addition to the Passover ritual and functioned as an interpretation of what Jesus was doing.

In the same way the words and actions of Jesus with the wine follow the rubrics for the blessing or thanksgiving after the meal. The head of the household sat up again from his reclining position, took the cup of wine, and said the blessing over it in the name

[10]For a more detailed account of the Passover ritual see *Eucharistic Words*, 84–88, and R. J. Karris, "The Gospel according to Luke," *NJBC*, 715.

of his table companions who made it their own by saying "Amen."
Then he passed the cup to everyone present. The New Testament
echoes this very closely in the phrases "taking the cup" and "having given thanks," "he gave it to them." Paul and Luke even
specify that this took place "after supper." It is after he had given
the cup to them that the accounts continue with the phrase, "he
said," so that, as with the bread, it was during the sharing of the
cup that Jesus spoke the words of interpretation which were, once
again, an addition to the Passover ritual. Immediately following
the blessing after the Passover meal, the "Hallel" was sung, a col-
lection of psalms. Mark follows this sequence when he ends the
Last Supper with the singing of "the Passover hymn" (Mark
14:26).

Before looking at the words of interpretation which Jesus spoke
over the bread and wine, it is important to note a second context
within which the Last Supper must be understood. This meal of
Jesus with his disciples, however special it was, was not an isolated
event, but was the last in a long series of meals which they shared
together. Such table fellowship was a sign of fellowship of life.
Moreover, Jesus opened this fellowship to others, even to sinners
and outcasts, a practice which offended against the custom of the
day according to which such people were to be shunned (hence,
the accusations of the scribes and Pharisees against Jesus that he
"welcomes sinners and eats with them" [Luke 15:2; Mark 2:16]).
The ongoing celebration of the Lord's Supper in the early Christian communities, then, not only hearkened back to the Last Supper, but was also a continuation of their union and table fellowship
with Jesus and with one another. The farewell meal before Jesus'
death enhanced the reality and meaning of this fellowship.

It did this especially in Jesus' actions and words at the blessing
before and after the meal. These actions and words are preserved
for us in a variety of versions, all of which bear the marks of liturgical adaptation and editing on the part of the authors. We have already seen the versions of Paul and Mark. By way of comparison
Luke's version reads as follows:

> And taking bread, having given thanks, he broke it and gave it to
> them saying: "This is my body which is given for you. Do this in
> memory of me." And in the same way after supper the cup saying:
> "This cup [is] the new covenant in my blood which is poured out
> for you" (Luke 22:19-20).

Luke's version is closely related to Paul's as is Matthew's to Mark's, but compared to Mark, Matthew shows signs of the move from narrative to liturgy mentioned above:

> As they were eating Jesus, taking bread and having said the bless-ing, broke it and giving it to the disciples said: "Take, eat, this is my body." And taking the cup and having given thanks he gave it to them saying: "Drink of it all of you. For this is my blood of the covenant which is poured out for many to the forgiveness of sins" (Matt 26:26-28).

Matthew's liturgical commands "eat" and "drink" replace Mark's narrative, "and they all drank of it."

No one version, then, can be said to report the actual words of Jesus. But the common core which all the versions have in com-mon reflects the substance of what Jesus said and did.[11] As the bread was being distributed Jesus said: "This" [is] "my body." The "is" became explicit in the Greek translations, but the original Aramaic or Hebrew characteristically would not have had such a copulative verb. Likewise, as the cup of wine was being passed, Jesus said: "This" [is] "my blood of the covenant" or "the covenant in my blood" [which is] "for many." What would these words have meant to the disciples hearing them as the bread and wine were being shared among them?

An interpretation of the unleavened bread and perhaps also of the wine would have been given already during the Passover lit-urgy, but now Jesus reinterprets them in relation to his own per-son. The reference of the bread and wine to his own person is expressed in the twin concept "body and blood" or "flesh and blood," which in its cultic usage bears the sacrificial meaning of the separation of the flesh and blood in the killing of the sacrificial animal.[12] In applying this concept to himself Jesus is speaking of his body and blood, of himself, as a sacrifice. The bread that is bro-ken and given points to his body, just as the wine that is poured out points to his blood. "Jesus used bread and wine to represent his coming death," says Meier, and continues:

---

[11]See Jeremias' construction in *Eucharistic Words,* 173. Similar is the con-struction of Meier in "Jesus," *NJBC,* 1327.

[12]*Eucharistic Words,* 221–222.

Jesus therefore interpreted his death as the (sacrificial? atoning?) means by which God would restore the covenant with Israel at Sinai.[13]

Jesus' words and actions at the supper, then, point to his coming death as the new Passover sacrifice and to himself as the new Paschal lamb whose blood is to seal a new covenant. In the mention of Jesus' blood the disciples would have recognized the allusion to the sacrifice of animals and the sprinkling of their blood by which the Sinai covenant was sealed at the time of Moses (Exod 24: 3-8). The mention of the covenant, which Paul and Luke call a "new covenant," hearkens back to the promise of a new covenant in Jeremiah (Jer 31:31).

The interpretation of Jesus' death as a sacrifice is strengthened by another aspect of Jesus' words which varies in the different traditions. In Paul the word "body" is followed by "which is for you," and in Luke by "which is given for you." This is missing in Mark and Matthew, but in Mark the word "blood" is followed by "which is poured out for many," and in Matthew by "which is poured out for many to the forgiveness of sins." Paul has no such comment after "blood," whereas Luke has a phrase similar to Mark's, "which is poured out for you." The term "to pour out" or "to shed" blood is taken from the language of sacrifice and alludes to a passage in Isaiah on the suffering servant who "poured out his life to death" (Isa 53:12). These phrases too, then, link Jesus' words and actions at the supper to his approaching death.

A striking feature of the passion narrative in John's Gospel and his account of the Last Supper is the absence of any mention of these words and actions of Jesus with the bread and wine. This is surprising not only because of their presence in all the other Gospels and in Paul, but also because of the celebration of the Lord's Supper in the Christian communities from the earliest times. This fact is less surprising, however, when it is noticed that John actually has the equivalent in an earlier section of his Gospel (John 6:51b-59). Indeed, then it is the similarity of this passage with the Last Supper narratives that becomes striking. The common core of the latter tradition over the bread reads, "This is my body," and John, paraphrasing "this" to fit into his context, reads, "The bread which I shall give is my flesh" (John 6:51). John's "flesh" perhaps echoes the

[13]"Jesus," *NJBC*, 1327.

semitic original more closely than the word "body," and when he adds after flesh, "for the life of the world," he is echoing the "for many" or "for you" of the other traditions.

Moreover, it has been suggested that these verses in John's Gospel have their origin in the liturgical celebration of the Lord's Supper in the Johannine community.[14] In this case they represent an independent version of Jesus' words of interpretation over the bread at the Last Supper. This passage in John goes on to speak not only of eating the "flesh" of the Son of Man, but also of drinking his "blood." It also says that this flesh is "real food" and this blood is "real drink" which give "eternal life" (John 6:53-55). This elaboration of the Lord's words could even represent the kind of exposition that would have accompanied the memorial of the Lord's Supper and the proclamation of his death in the liturgical celebrations of the early Christian communities.[15]

So far we have been considering the words of the Lord which are common to all the Last Supper traditions or, as in the "for many" phrase, which appear with variations. But present in only some of the traditions is the command of the Lord: "Do this in memory of me." Paul records the command twice, after Jesus' words of interpretation of both the bread and the wine. Luke has the same command but only once, after the words of interpretation of the bread. It is not mentioned in either Mark or Matthew. The fact that the command is found only in the Pauline-Lukan branch of the tradition could be thought to argue against its historicity and to suggest that the regular meals of the community were not in response to the command of Jesus to repeat the rite. Rather, the practice itself would have given rise to the command being placed on the lips of Jesus. A consideration of the meaning of the command can perhaps throw light on this question.

As is clear from the earliest practice of the Christian communities, the phrase "do this" was understood not just as a recital of Jesus' words, but as a repetition of the entire rite of blessing or thanksgiving over the bread and wine, that is, of Jesus' actions as well as his words. In what sense was Jesus to be "remembered" in this repetition? It can be interpreted to mean that the memory

[14]See Pheme Perkins, "The Gospel according to John," *NJBC*, 962, and *Eucharistic Words*, 107–108.
[15]See *Eucharistic Words*, 106–108.

of Jesus was kept alive among his disciples by this rite, somewhat after the analogy of the Hellenistic practice of commemorative meals for the dead. But Jeremias sees another possible interpretation, one which finds its analogy rather among Jewish practices in Palestine.[16] He points to the Jewish practice whereby something is presented before God, for example, a bequest or a prayer, with the purpose of having God "remember" something or someone. God's "remembering," moreover, is understood as creative and effective: when God "remembers" his covenant, this means that he is fulfilling the covenant promises, and when he "remembers" the iniquities of Babylon, this means that he is delivering his judgment upon them.

A further and more pertinent example of this is found in an ancient Passover prayer in which God is asked "to remember the Messiah." In light of the above this is a prayer for the appearance of the Messiah, for the fulfillment of the promise of the kingdom and the coming of the Parousia. If, indeed, there are resonances of this practice in the command to repeat the Last Supper rite as a remembrance of Jesus, the rite is performed and presented before God as an entreaty that *God* remember Jesus, that is, that God will hasten the day of his second coming and the consummation of the kingdom. The command looks not just to the past death of Jesus, but also looks to the future and takes on an eschatological dimension in its longing for his second coming.

Jeremias sees support for this interpretation of "remembrance" in Paul's comment after he reports the command to repeat the rite: "For as often as you eat this bread and drink this cup, you proclaim the Lord's death until he comes" (1 Cor 11:26).[17] Coming as it does immediately after, "Do this, as often as you drink it, in memory of me," the verse says that the command is fulfilled by eating the bread and drinking the cup and proclaiming the Lord's death "until he comes." The latter need not be read only as a temporal reference, stipulating the duration of the command. "Until he comes" also has the connotation of the purpose and goal of the remembrance and the proclamation of his death, namely, that the goal may be reached, that he may come.[18] The remembrance

---

[16]See *Eucharistic Words*, 238–252.

[17]*Eucharistic Words*, 252–255.

[18]This meaning of "until" has an obvious parallel in English, for example, to keep asking someone for something until they finally grant it.

and proclamation of his death would then be related to the liturgical prayer *maranatha,* "Come Lord," by which the community prayed for and asked God "to remember" the eschatological coming of the Lord. Despite the doubts mentioned above about the historicity of the command, in this eschatological context it can perhaps be more probably traced back to Jesus himself at the supper.

However that may be, Jesus does make a clear allusion to God's eschatological fulfillment of his promises in the three Gospel accounts of the Last Supper. Luke places it at the very beginning of the meal: "For I say to you that I shall not eat it until it is fulfilled in the kingdom of God" (Luke 22:16). He then repeats it again at the first cup of wine: "For I say to you that from now on I shall not drink from the fruit of the vine until the kingdom of God comes" (Luke 22:18). Mark and Matthew have this allusion to the coming of the kingdom only once, following the blessing after the meal toward the very end of the celebration. Mark's version reads: "Truly I say to you that I shall not drink again of the fruit of the vine until that day when I drink it new in the kingdom of God" (Mark 14:25). The so-called "eschatological prospect" appears, then, in both major traditions of the supper narrative. Both traditions portray Jesus as being aware of his imminent death and as approaching his death steadfast in his hope for the final coming of God's kingdom.

Luke's positioning of the kingdom allusion at the very beginning of the meal raises the further question, whether he is implying that Jesus himself abstained from food and drink at this final meal. Jeremias thinks that he is, especially in view of the further statement he has Jesus making as they gather for the meal: "I have earnestly desired to eat this Passover with you before I suffer" (Luke 22:15).[19] This particular use of the verb "desire" occurs in three other passages in Luke (Luke 15:16; 16:21; 17:22) and in only one other New Testament passage (Matt 13:17). In all of these instances it seems to mean an unfulfilled desire, for example, when it is said of the prodigal son that "he would have been glad to fill his belly with the pods the pigs were eating, but no one gave him anything" (Luke 15:16). If this is also the meaning of "desire" in the Last Supper narrative, then Jesus is saying that he would very gladly have eaten the Passover lamb with his disciples. But,

[19] See *Eucharistic Words,* 207–212.

as he explains in the following verse, he will not eat "until it is fulfilled in the kingdom of God." Two verses later he says the same of the wine when he tells the disciples to "take this and share it among yourselves."

If, indeed, this is what Luke meant in these verses, what could explain the unusual action of Jesus in abstaining from food and drink during the meal? There is abundant evidence in Jewish literature for the practice of such abstinence and renunciation,[20] but perhaps the most likely explanation comes from early Christian practice. It was the custom in the early Jewish Christian communities to fast while the Jews were celebrating their Passover meal, and this for the sake of their lost brothers and sisters and for those who were persecuting them. This could perhaps reveal the motive for fast and abstinence by Jesus at the Last Supper. Jesus' renunciation was his final gesture for the sake of his people who had rejected him. If that is the case, Jesus' abstinence at the Last Supper would explain the origin of the custom of fasting at Passover in the early Jewish Christian communities.[21] Whatever the merits of this interpretation, Jesus does relate his final meal with his disciples to the eschatological fulfillment of God's promise of the kingdom when he will again eat and drink with them.

The story of the Last Supper, then, as narrated in the Gospels and Paul and as celebrated in the early liturgy has a three-fold focus. It looks to the past, to its origins in the Passover meal of the Jews. It looks to the present, to the death of Jesus, which is symbolized and represented in the actions and words of Jesus with the bread and wine. It looks to the future, to the final coming of the kingdom and the eternal eschatological banquet. According to the analysis of Jungmann we examined earlier,[22] when the early Christian community followed the Lord's command to "Do this in memory of me," they saw in this memorial of his words and actions not *a* mystery, but *the* mystery of their faith. It is this aspect of the Eucharistic meal as a summary and recapitulation of the whole of Christian faith that we wish to examine further.

---

[20] *Eucharistic Words,* 212–216.
[21] *Eucharistic Words,* 124–125, 216–218.
[22] Introduction, 5–6.

# 2

# Faith and History

Seeing the Last Supper against the background of the Jewish Passover meal throws much light on the meaning of many of the details recorded in the New Testament accounts of the supper, meaning which would have been quite obvious to early Jewish Christians. Remembering that the Passover was a *ritual* meal can also throw light on how they would have understood this aspect of the Last Supper. At Passover the Jewish people remembered and celebrated in ritual something which had actually happened in their past history. They remembered the Exodus event when God had acted in Moses to liberate his people from the slavery of Egypt. This past event was remembered not just for the sake of the past but also for the sake of the present and the future. The God who had acted for them in the past was still present and active in their history and would one day bring about their final liberation in the coming of the kingdom. The ritual words and actions of the Passover meal, then, pointed beyond themselves to history, to what had happened in the past, and to a future that was still to come.

The first Jewish Christians believed that God was again active in their history in the person of Jesus of Nazareth. They, too, memorialized this event in a meal, the celebration of the Lord's Supper which eventually replaced the Passover celebration in their communities. But this "new covenant" meal was no less related to history than was that of the Mosaic covenant. It proclaimed "the death of the Lord," his real death on Calvary, and was to continue to do so until that future event when he would "come again."

For the Christian faith no less than the Jewish faith is a historical religion in the sense that it is not about eternal truths but about things that God has actually done in history and things that God is yet to do. Christian faith is not about God in God's eternal self but about God as related to the world, God present and active in history, past, present, and future.

This explains why the very first Jewish Christian communities did not see themselves as having entered into a new religion, but as having entered upon a new phase of Jewish history. We read in the Acts of the Apostles, for instance, that the early disciples of Jesus "kept up their daily attendance at the Temple (Acts 2:46) and that Peter and John continued to go up to the Temple for the "hour of prayer" (Acts 3:1). It was in the Jewish synagogues of the Diaspora scattered throughout the Hellenistic world that Paul preached his message about Jesus (Acts 13:5, 15; 14:1). They still saw themselves, then, as members of the Jewish religion, indeed, as the true Jewish believers who had recognized God's action in the historical events of Jesus' life. But in addition to attendance at the Temple and synagogue their fellowship with Jesus and with each other was expressed and strengthened by "breaking bread in private houses" and "sharing meals" (Acts 2:46). How was this ritual activity in which bread was broken and wine was shared in order to proclaim the Lord's death until he comes related to the new phase of history which he had inaugurated?

The question is important because it is possible for ritual and cultic activity to become separated from history and real life and to assume an ahistorical life of its own. The Letter to the Hebrews, quoting Psalm 40 about the Old Testament ritual sacrifices, says that it is not such "sacrifice and oblation" that God "desires or takes delight in," but in Jesus who came to do God's will by offering his own body in self-sacrifice (Heb 10:5-10). His was not the ritual sacrifice of "the blood of goats and calves," but the real sacrifice of "his own blood" (Heb 9:12). Psalm 51 also speaks of ritual sacrifices when it says that God "does not take delight in sacrifice" and "would not accept it." Rather "a broken spirit" and "a wounded heart" is the sacrifice that the Lord "will not despise" (Ps 51:16-17). Ritual sacrifice separated from real sacrifice, from life and history, can become empty ritualism. Like the ritual of the Passover meal, then, Jesus' ritual activity at the Last Supper points beyond itself to real history, to the history of his own life that was at that moment reaching its climactic point. For it was of this history and this life that he spoke in his ritual words and actions with the bread and wine.

In this sense the ritual itself represented and was a real symbol of what was actually happening and was about to happen in the real historical life of Jesus, who was himself symbolized in the ritual. What does Jesus say about himself in his ritual symbolic action? According to the common elements in the various traditions of the Last Supper narrative, Jesus said that the bread that was broken was his body or his flesh and that the wine was his blood of the covenant which is poured out for many. In these words Jesus asserts an identification between, on the one hand, his action with the bread and wine which was the symbol, and, on the other hand, his real flesh and blood which were the symbolized. What grounds the truth of this identification? What makes his action with the bread and wine a real symbol of his flesh and blood? What connects the ritual action with the action of his real life and his real history?

To answer these questions we must look to history, to the historical Jesus of Nazareth. When Jesus actually gave his body and blood as he gave the bread and wine at the supper, when his body was actually broken as the bread was broken, and when his blood was actually poured out as the wine was poured out, then the identification Jesus asserted between the two became very real. The ritual at the Last Supper really expresses what actually happened historically on Calvary. His giving the bread and the wine became real symbols of his flesh and blood because of what he did the following day: he actually gave his flesh and blood, his life, as food and drink, that is, as the source of life for others. The words and actions of Jesus at the supper, then, depend on what he did on Calvary for their reality and truth. The ritual action finds in Jesus' historical action its real fulfillment.

This is clear if one supposes for a moment that the Last Supper ritual had not been followed by the historical events of the following day. What meaning or truth could the ritual words and actions of Jesus have had? Without Calvary what he said of his body and blood through the symbolism of bread broken and wine poured out would not have been true. The bread and wine would not have been real symbols of his body and blood. Jesus fills the symbol of the bread and wine with himself and makes it a real symbol of his body and blood only through what he did the following day. The ritual action at the supper finds its reality and truth in history, in what Jesus did on Calvary. It is on Calvary that his flesh becomes "real food" and his blood "real drink," as John expresses it (John 6:55), for only then does it become a source of life by really being "given" and "poured out for many." Just as the Passover meal points to the real event of the Exodus, so too does the symbolic action of the Last Supper find its meaning in the real events of Jesus' life and death.

The symbolic action that Jesus chose expresses that meaning more graphically than words alone could have done. His death was, to be sure, something inflicted upon him, something that he had to suffer and endure, but the symbol proclaims more than that. It says that his death was also his own action, that he freely gave his life for others. It thus proclaims his death as his own free act of love and compassion. In doing so it sounds a theme that occurs frequently in the Gospel narratives about Jesus and relates his death to the life that had preceded it. The symbol portrays Jesus as dying just as he had always lived. Just as the Last Supper itself hearkens back to the table fellowship Jesus had established during his life, so too does the symbolic action at the meal point backward to his life as well as forward to his death the following day. A brief look at the theme of compassion in the Gospel narratives shows that the symbol speaks not just of how Jesus died, but also of how he lived.

The Synoptic Gospels introduce many aspects of the varied ministry of Jesus on the note of compassion. The aspect most closely connected with the symbolism of the Last Supper has to do with Jesus feeding his people. Mark records two such incidents and associates both of them with the compassion of Jesus. The first portrays Jesus and his disciples setting off by boat for a private place in search of rest and quiet, but the people pursued them. When Jesus saw the crowd, "He had compassion on them because they were like sheep without a shepherd" (Mark 6:34), and at the end of a day of teaching them during which they had not eaten, Jesus provided food for the entire five thousand. Mark introduces the second such incident on the same note. Looking on the "huge crowd" that was following him, Jesus called his disciples and said: "I have compassion for these people; they have been with me now for three days and have nothing to eat" (Mark 8:2). The story ends again with Jesus feeding the multitude because of the compassion he has for them.

The details of both stories are so similar that they are perhaps two versions of the same incident.[1] These details would have struck many chords familiar to the original hearers of the stories. They would have recognized an echo of God's feeding his people during their wandering in the desert and of his promise of the kingdom and the messianic banquet to come. There is also an obvious allusion to the Last Supper when, before distributing the bread, Jesus "said the blessing and broke the loaves" (Mark 6:41; see also 8:6). Whatever the nature of the original event was, and it is narrated in all four Gospels (Matt 14:15-21; Luke 9:12-17; John 6:1-15), Mark's version of the story portrays Jesus as one who was moved by compassion to satisfy the hunger of his people.

Matthew's two accounts of Jesus feeding the multitude follow Mark very closely, but his report of the first introduces another aspect of Jesus' ministry that is also associated with his compassion. As in Mark the crowds pursue Jesus who had withdrawn to a lonely place, and when he saw them he "had compassion on them, and he cured those of them who were sick" (Matt 14:14). Matthew associates Jesus' compassion with the sick as well as with the hungry, and he does this elsewhere as well:

> Jesus went about all the cities and villages, teaching in their synagogues and announcing the good news of the kingdom, and healing every disease and every infirmity. When he saw the crowds he had compassion on them, because they were harrassed and helpless, like sheep without a shepherd (Matt 9:35-36).

Matthew also makes explicit in this passage that the compassion of Jesus manifested in healing the sick and feeding the hungry is part of his "announcing the good news of the kingdom."

The passage portrays Jesus not only as announcing the kingdom but also inaugurating it, as does the story of the two blind men whom Jesus encounters as he leaves the city of Jericho. His attention is attracted by their shouts and he asks what they would have him do for them. When they ask that they might see, Jesus was "moved by compassion and touched their eyes," and at once their sight was restored (Matt 20:34). Commentators point out

---

[1]See Daniel Harrington, "The Gospel According to Mark," *NJBC*, 610, 613.

that the root of the Greek word for compassion is derived from the word for "entrails" or "guts," emphasizing the depth of Jesus' feeling for the people who are wandering in darkness like sheep without a shepherd.[2]

Two of Matthew's parables of the kingdom focus on the theme of compassion. In the first Jesus tells the story of the servant who could not pay his debt to his master and was to be sold to meet the debt. When he begs for patience, his master "was moved with compassion" and remitted the debt. But the servant refuses to treat a fellow-servant in debt to him with the same compassion, and therefore loses the forgiveness he had received. So too, concludes Jesus, "will my heavenly father deal with you, unless you each forgive your brother from your hearts" (Matt 18:23-35). The second parable makes compassion the norm for entrance into the kingdom. When the Son of Man comes on the last day, says the parable, he will divide all peoples into two groups. Those on his right he welcomes into the kingdom, for they showed compassion to those who were hungry or thirsty, to those who were strangers or naked, to those who were sick or in prison, and in doing so they were showing compassion to the Son of Man himself. Those on his left he tells to depart, for they failed to show compassion in those situations, and what they did not do for the least of their brothers and sisters they did not do for the Son of Man (Matt 25:31-46).

Luke, too, speaks of Jesus' compassion in a variety of contexts. In one he tells the story of Jesus and his disciples approaching the town of Nain where they met a funeral procession. A widowed mother was on the way to bury her only son. "When the Lord saw her he had compassion on her," and stopping the procession he bade the boy rise up and gave him back to his mother (Luke 7:11-15). Sometimes it is in the parables of Jesus that Luke makes compassion a central theme. Among the most famous of his parables is the story of the good Samaritan. It tells the story of a man who had fallen in with robbers and was beaten and left half-dead on the road side. A priest and a Levite passed him by, and then a third traveler came along:

> But a Samaritan who was making the journey came upon him, and when he saw him he was moved by compassion. He went up and

[2]See Benedict Viviano, "The Gospel According to Matthew," *NJBC*, 650.

bandaged his wounds, bathing them with oil and wine (Luke 10:33-34).

His compassion moved him to treat the man's wounds and bring him to an inn until he recovered. The story ends with the admonition, "Go and do as he did."

Some of the parables portray another manifestation of Jesus' compassion, his compassion for sinners, the central motif in the parable of the prodigal son. After telling the story of the younger son taking his inheritance and going off to a far country and then repenting and returning to his father, Jesus describes their reunion:

> But while he was still a long way off his father saw him, and he had compassion on him. He ran to meet him, flung his arms around him, and kissed him (Luke 15:20).

This parable is preceded by two shorter ones making the same point. The first tells of the shepherd who leaves his ninety-nine sheep to go in search of one which was lost (Luke 15:4-7), and the second of the woman who lights the lamp and sweeps the house until she has found the silver piece that was lost (Luke 15:8-10). Both parables end on the note of the joy that is felt in heaven for the sinner who was lost but is found.

All three of these parables are provoked by the accusation made against Jesus by the Pharisees and doctors of the Law that he "welcomes sinners and eats with them" (Luke 15:2). Jesus welcomes everyone to his table fellowship as a sign of the kingdom and a foretaste of the messianic banquet. In Luke's Gospel Jesus also uses parables to illustrate the lack of compassion. He tells the story of the rich man who dined lavishly every day but denied even the scraps from his table to the poor man Lazarus. When he dies and finds himself in torment, he asks Abraham for compassion, but it is denied him because in life he had not shown compassion to others (Luke 16:19-31). Toward the end of Jesus' life Luke presents one of his most poignant portraits of the compassion of Jesus. As he approaches Jerusalem on what is to be his last visit which ends with his death, the sight of the city moves him to compassion: "When he came in sight of the city, he wept over it and said, 'If only you had known, on this great day, the way that leads to peace'" (Luke 19:41-42).

The Gospel portraits of Jesus as a man of compassion as well as his parables on compassion are reflected in his teaching. In Mark and Matthew Jesus is asked what is the "first" or the "greatest" commandment in the Law. In both instances he answers that the first commandment is to love God, and the second is like it: love your neighbor as yourself. In Mark Jesus says: "There is no other commandment greater than these" (Mark 12:31), and in Matthew he says: "Everything in the Law and the prophets hangs on these two commandments" (Matt 22:40). In Luke the question is phrased differently: "Master, what must I do to inherit eternal life?" But the answer is the same, to which Jesus adds: "Do that and you will live" (Luke 10:25-28).

Looking at this variety of materials in the Synoptic Gospels, whether it be the portraits they paint of Jesus in his attitude and behavior toward others in need of food or healing or forgiveness, or the parables he told, or the commandments he taught, it is clear that love and compassion are a central theme in his life and ministry. The ritual words and actions of Jesus at the Last Supper, which pointed so graphically to his death the following day when he gave his life for others, also point back to his earlier history. It is John's Gospel which, in its account of the passion and death of Jesus, makes quite explicit this link between Jesus' death and his life which led up to it.

John introduces the passion narrative by saying that what Jesus is about to do in his passion and death continues and completes what he had been doing during his life:

> Now before the feast of the Passover, when Jesus knew that his hour had come to depart out of this world to the Father, having loved his own who were in the world, he loved them unto the end (John 13:1).

John tells the story of Jesus' death as the story of his love for his own, a love he had already shown them, but now he was to love them "unto the end." Although he does not include in his account of the Last Supper the ritual expression of this love in the symbolism of the bread and wine, he replaces it with an equally telling symbol of this love in word and action.

During the supper, says John, "Jesus rose from table, laid aside his garments, and taking a towel, tied it round him" (John 13:4). Then he poured water into a basin and, to the astonishment of the disciples, began to wash their feet. It was the custom in Jesus' day that the host of a meal would have one of his servants wash the feet of the guests as a sign of hospitality.[3] On an earlier occasion Jesus pointed out to a Pharisee named Simon that he had received no such hospitality from him when he arrived for a meal, but that a woman who was a sinner came forward and washed his feet with her tears and dried them with her hair, and Jesus saw this as a sign of "her great love" (Luke 7:36-50). Here at the Last Supper Jesus uses the footwashing as a sign of his own love for his disciples.

"Do you understand what I have done for you?" he asks after resuming his place at table. He who is their master and lord has assumed the role of servant, saying thereby something about the nature of lordship and the nature of love. Washing their feet is like a parable in action which says that to love is to serve, and the one who thus loves is true lord and master. The parable becomes real in his historical action the following day. Like his actions with the bread and wine, washing their feet represents the great act of love he is to perform on Calvary by giving his life for them. But the parable must also become real in their lives: "I have set you an example: you are to do as I have done for you." If they have heard and understood the truth of the parable, happy will they be if they "do it," just as Jesus has done it in life as well as in death (John 13:12-17).

John elaborates further on the meaning of Jesus' death in the "farewell discourses" that follow in his narrative of the Last Supper. What Jesus did in death is not only the continuation of what he did in life, but also its climax and culmination: "Greater love than this no man has, than that a man lay down his life for his friends" (John 15:13). Loving "unto the end" means, then, not only up to the final moment, but also loving to the limits of which love is capable. For in giving his life, Jesus gave not just this or that part of himself, but his whole self. There was nothing more to give, no remainder left ungiven. Moreover, giving one's life is the final and definitive giving, the giving that admits of no change or taking back. In dying Jesus did finally and fully what he had been doing all through life.

From this perspective one can see that when John speaks of the hour of Jesus' passion and death as the hour of his "glory" (John 12:23), the glory does not simply begin after the death of Jesus.

[3]See Pheme Perkins, "The Gospel According to John," *NJBC,* 973.

In his ironic portrait of Jesus' death, the moment of his dying is itself the moment when he was most fully alive. For death was not just something inflicted upon him, something he suffered and endured, but also, as an act of love, it was something he did freely. In dying he did most fully and completely what he had been doing throughout his life. In this sense it was at the moment of death that he was most completely free and most fully alive, for it was then that he loved most perfectly. The paradox of Jesus' Cross is that it is a sign not just of his death, but also of life, of life even in death, of life that death cannot destroy. In John's ironic portrait, the hour of Jesus' passion and death *is* the hour of his glory.

As with the symbolism of the bread and wine in the Synoptic Gospels, which points backward to the life of Jesus as well as forward to his death, so too has John anticipated his portrait of Jesus' death as his greatest act of love in his portrait of Jesus' earlier life as a man of compassion. This note is sounded most clearly in the story of Jesus and Lazarus (John 11:1-44), which emphasizes at several points the deep love that Jesus felt for his friend. Jesus was at some distance when he received news that Lazarus was ill, and when he arrived to find Lazarus dead and his sisters weeping, "he was deeply moved." When he too wept, the others said: "See how he loved him." Then Jesus went to the tomb and there, John says, "he was deeply moved again." All of these details are part of the prelude to Jesus calling Lazarus forth from the tomb. They emphasize the love and compassion Jesus felt for his friend, and the raising of Lazarus is a sign of the life that Jesus' final act of love will bestow on others.

This theme is also present in parable, for example, in the story of the good shepherd (John 10:1-18). When Jesus told this parable, says John, the people "did not understand what he meant by it," so Jesus explains that a hireling abandons the sheep in the face of danger because he has no concern for them. But a good shepherd is one who lays down his life for his sheep. Then he says that he is that shepherd who knows his sheep and is ready to lay down his life for them. He does this in order that they "may have life, and have it in all its fullness." Shortly thereafter Jesus uses the image of the grain of wheat to make the same point:

> In truth, in very truth I tell you, a grain of wheat remains a solitary grain unless it falls into the ground and dies; but if it dies, it bears much fruit (John 12:24).

Both the parable and the image point forward to the death of Jesus where his life reaches its climax and fulfillment.

Finally, John has his own version of Jesus' teaching about the "first" or "greatest" commandment; he calls it a "new" commandment. He places it at several points during the "farewell discourses" at the Last Supper. On taking leave of his disciples Jesus gives them a single commandment: "I give you a new commandment: love one another; as I have loved you, so you are to love one another" (John 13:34). Indeed, this is how "all will know that you are my disciples." A little later Jesus speaks of his disciples not as "servants" but as "friends," and then twice repeats his command to them "to love one another as I have loved you" (John 15:11-17). In John's version the two commandments of the Synoptics have become one, and Jesus makes his own love the model and norm for his disciples.

We have tried to see how the various accounts of the Last Supper, both the words and actions of Jesus with the bread and wine in the Synoptic Gospels and the footwashing in John, are not separate incidents to be understood in isolation. Rather, as representational symbols they speak preeminently of the death of Jesus, but also of his life. For as John especially tries to make clear, Jesus' living and dying are moments in a single process: Jesus did fully in death what he had been doing all through life. But it is also clear from the variety of the narratives that they are not a history or a biography of Jesus' life and death. They are rather theological portraits which have been shaped and molded by the theological perspectives and concerns of the authors and by the different oral traditions from which they emerged. The Gospels are, and were intended to be, books of faith. They record the faith of the early Christian communities in Jesus of Nazareth. As John puts it, he has written his Gospel "in order that you may come to believe that Jesus is the Christ, the Son of God . . ." (John 20:31). A literal or fundamentalist reading of the Gospels can miss the real point that the narrative is making.

But it is equally true, nevertheless, that the early Christian communities placed their faith in an actual historical person who evoked that faith by the way he lived and the way he died. Christianity is a historical religion in the sense that it believes God is present and acts in history, most particularly in the history of Jesus of Nazareth. Its symbols and texts are important not because they "contain" certain truths but because they point to and disclose God's presence and action in particular persons and particular events. That is why the Last Supper symbols which speak of the historical Jesus are so important. They afford us a glimpse into the historical life and death of Jesus of Nazareth, a glimpse of what he was actually like and what he actually did, and tell us what it was about him that evoked faith in him. The early Christians did not place their faith in symbols or texts but in him of whom the symbols and texts spoke. The symbols and the texts were expressions of their faith, written, as John says above, that others might come to believe in him.

When the symbols and texts are dissociated from history and Christian faith loses its roots in the life and death of Jesus of Nazareth, it is then understood in a more gnostic or docetic way in the sense that history does not embody divine presence and divine activity. God docs not "become flesh," as the Prologue to John's Gospel expresses it, and does not thereby become present and active within the confines of the world and history. God operates rather in a separate, supernatural realm, knowledge of which one has through the truths revealed by Jesus and contained in Scripture. Faith is no longer an encounter with the person of Jesus and the historical reality of his life and death, but a knowledge of the truths he has revealed.

When Christian faith becomes dissociated from the past history of Jesus of Nazareth, it also becomes dissociated from history in the present. It does not find God present and active in the world and historical reality today, but in another and different salvation history. The salvation it offers, like its image of Jesus, is docetic. Salvation is not embodied in the historical reality of the present but has its own invisible and separate history, running its course independently of the course of secular history in a world apart. Such an understanding of Christian faith is inevitably dualistic, dividing matter from spirit, body from soul, natural from supernatural, secular from sacred, and God from the world. These divisions are at the root of the docetic image of Jesus according to which he only appeared to be flesh and to dwell among us. Faith encounters this docetic Jesus in a religious realm apart from the world and its history.

Such a docetic understanding of Jesus would affect the meaning of his symbolic actions with the bread and wine at the Last

Supper. They would not be related to the historical Jesus, to his actual living and dying, for Jesus would not have lived a human life nor died a human death. They would have their own self-contained ritual and cultic meaning. Unlike the Passover meal that it replaced in Christian communities, which celebrates the presence and action of God in history in the Exodus event, the Lord's Supper would celebrate the Lord's presence in the ritual and cult itself, not in history, neither the history of the past nor of the present. Jesus would be present in bread broken and wine poured out not because he made them real symbols of himself in his historical action on Calvary, but because of the cultic action itself which he "instituted" for this purpose.

To prevent the Jesus of history from being replaced by a Jesus of ritual and cultic mysteries, the reality and meaning of the ritual and cultic action must have its roots in the life and death of the Jesus of history of whom it is the symbol. As the symbol itself proclaims, moreover, his history did not end with his death.

# 3

# The Paschal Mystery

When the first Christians proclaimed the Lord's death "until he comes," it is clear that they saw his death not as an end, but as a beginning. This conviction came to expression in the resurrection symbol, the symbol of the dawning of a new age that had its beginnings in Jesus when "God raised him to life again" (Acts 2:24). The Cross was significant, then, not as an isolated event in itself, but because it was the passage into this new life and new age. Hence the Cross must be understood in the larger context of resurrection and kingdom. Likewise, however, the passage into this life lies precisely and only through the Cross, so that resurrection and kingdom must be understood in the context of the Cross. Cross and resurrection are two sides of one coin, and together they form the single mystery of the life of Jesus, the Paschal mystery of his passage through death to new life.

The significance of the Cross has not always been seen precisely in its relationship to resurrection and as forming a single mystery with the resurrection. When the death of Jesus is not seen as the final and culminating moment of his life and as the passage into new life, that is, when his death is separated both from his earthly life and the new life of the resurrection, its significance must be found in some value that is attached to his death itself. Against the background of the Old Testament, images and analogies for such an understanding of his death lie readily at hand in Jewish sacrificial practices. Among these practices was the offering to God of a "sacrifice of expiation," the ritual killing of an animal or, in the case of poor people, of birds as a way of propitiating God for some offense that was committed.[1] The desired effect of the sacrifice was atonement for sin and reconciliation with God. So understood, Jesus would have been the sacrificial victim whose death "for many" would have atoned for their sins and reconciled them with God. Paul uses this image when he speaks of Jesus as "the means of expiating sin by his sacrificial death" (Rom 3:25).

Another image found in Paul is that of "redemption," thought to be derived from the practice in antiquity of the manumission or liberation of slaves through the payment of a ransom. For example, Paul says that in Jesus we have been "set free" (1 Cor 1:31), and that Jesus "sacrificed himself to win freedom for all mankind" (1 Tim 2:6).[2] The same image appears in Mark and Matthew when Jesus says that, "The Son of Man did not come to be served, but to serve, and to give his life as a ransom for many" (Mark 10:45; Matt 20:28). According to this image, the death of Jesus would have been the price or ransom paid for the redemption of all people from the bondage of sin.

At a much later period of reflection on the meaning of the death of Jesus on the cross, Anselm of Canterbury in the eleventh century devised a theory of "satisfaction" to show the meaning of Jesus' death. In this instance the background is not Jewish religious thought, but the feudal society of Anselm's time with its social ranks and levels of dignity. A serf at the bottom of the social ladder could adequately satisfy or make up for an offense committed against a fellow serf, but not if the person offended was someone of higher dignity like a king. How much greater is the distance which separates sinful humankind from the infinite majesty of God. This reflection offers an answer to the question why God became man and gave his life on the cross. If adequate satisfaction were to be offered to the divine majesty and the scales of justice and order were to be set right, the one offering the satisfaction had to be of equal dignity with God and at the same time had to be one with humankind by whom the satisfaction had to be offered. Because

[1] On Jewish sacrifices see J. Castelot and A. Cody, "Religious Institutions of Israel," *NJBC,* 1268–1273.

[2] Paul uses other images besides those mentioned here to speak of the work of Christ, for example, reconciliation: "God was in Christ reconciling the world to himself" (2 Cor 5:19).

he was both God and man, only Jesus could offer adequate satisfaction for human sin.[3]

Common to both Anselm's theory of satisfaction and to the
notion of a sacrifice of expiation to throw light on the meaning
of Jesus' death is the idea that his death was somehow required
on God's part. The implication of both seems to be that, without
either expiation or satisfaction offered to God, the sin of humankind
could not or would not have been forgiven. God's love and forgiveness seem to be conditional and dependent on God receiving what
is God's due. A somewhat crude understanding could even think
of God undergoing a change of mind or heart toward humankind
as a result of Jesus' offering expiation or satisfaction for sin. In focus-
ing exclusively on the death of Jesus, moreover, neither theory sees
either the life of Jesus nor the resurrection as an intrinsic part of
the process of reconciliation. At most the resurrection signals in
an extrinsic way God's acceptance of the expiation or satisfaction
offered by his death or, in an equally extrinsic way, the resurrection verifies claims that Jesus supposedly made during his life.

But the New Testament offers other starting points for understanding the death of Jesus which do not see his death in isolation, but in relationship to his earlier life and to the resurrection.
John's Gospel sets the death of Jesus not in the context of expiation or satisfaction offered to God, but in the context of God's
action and God's love:

> God so loved the world that he gave his only Son, that everyone
> who has faith in him may not die but have eternal life. It was not
> to judge the world that God sent his Son into the world, but that
> through him the world might be saved (John 3:16-17).

John's starting point is not the anger of God requiring expiation
or the justice of God requiring satisfaction, but God's uncondi-
tional love. The Cross of Jesus is a moment in the process of God's
love becoming incarnate in the life and death of Jesus. If God's
love is the starting point, what is still outstanding, what must still
be accomplished, is not something on God's side, but that God
be loved in return. This Jesus did throughout his life, and especially in his death, as John says, by loving "unto the end." John

---

[3]See Anselm's *Cur Deus Homo* (Rome: Gregorian University Press, 1933).

finds the significance of Jesus' death, which is the culmination of his life, in the fullness of his love.

The notion of sacrifice, of course, is still present, but in the sense of self-sacrifice: "Greater love than this no one has, than that he lay down his life for his friends" (John 15:13). Such sacrifice is, indeed, the undoing of sin, for sin is the destruction of the bonds of love between humankind and God and among humankind, and love is the restoration of those bonds. In his "greater love" Jesus was at once the incarnation of God's love for the world and the human return of love to the Father. Jesus thereby not only accomplished, but *was* in his very person the reconciliation of God and the world, and this comes to expression in the resurrection symbol. The effect of Jesus' love and self-sacrifice, or what John calls the "fruit" of this love when he uses the image of the grain of wheat falling into the ground and dying (John 12:24), must be found not in propitiation or satisfaction on God's side of the relationship, but in its further effects on the human side. Paul points to these further effects when he speaks of the resurrection of Jesus as "the firstfruits of the harvest," to be followed "afterwards, at his coming," by "those who belong to Christ" (1 Cor 15:20-23).

The Letter to the Hebrews also stresses the new kind of sacrifice that inaugurates the new covenant: "The blood of his sacrifice is his own blood, not the blood of goats and calves" (Heb 9:12). In contrast to the ritual sacrifice on the Day of Atonement offered in the "sanctuary," Jesus "suffered outside the city gate," giving his life in an act of real sacrifice (Heb 13:11-12). But whereas John tells the story of the passion and death of Jesus as the story of his love, the author of Hebrews focuses on other aspects. He sees Jesus as the man of perfect obedience who has fulfilled the word of the psalmist: "I have come, O God, to do thy will" (Heb 10:7), and who has "learned obedience through the things which he suffered" (Heb 5:8). He also focuses on the faith of Jesus, for it was in faith that he accepted God's will. Hence we must keep "our eyes fixed on Jesus who is the pioneer and perfecter of our faith" (Heb 12:2).

When the sacrifice of the Cross is understood not in images of expiation, ransom, or satisfaction, but as the love and self-sacrifice of Jesus whose fruit is the new life of the resurrection, Cross and resurrection together portray Jesus doing the truth he taught his disciples: "For whoever would save his life will lose it, and whoever loses his life for my sake and the Gospel's will save it" (Mark

8:35). The paradox of "losing" and "saving" constitutes the single event and the single mystery of Cross and resurrection. Faith in the resurrection is not merely belief in life after death or in the immortality of the soul. Cross and resurrection together say not that life follows death, but that life follows love. Christian faith is not in the life, death, and resurrection of Jesus as separate events, but in the single mystery of Jesus whose life of love "unto the end" on the cross is the path to the new life of the resurrection and the new age of the kingdom.

We have been considering the resurrection in its relationship to the Cross as the object of Christian faith, but it is also presented in the New Testament as the ground of this faith. When Paul says that "if Christ was not raised, your faith is vain" (1 Cor 15:17), it is not only faith in the resurrection that is at stake, but also faith and hope in the kingdom Jesus preached and in the God who promised it. It was the experience of the risen Jesus which confirmed their faith, indeed finally brought them to the conversion of faith Jesus had called for: "The time has come; the kingdom of God is upon you; be converted and believe the good news" (Mark 1:15). The Gospels portray their conversion clearly enough. The story of the crucifixion of Jesus ends with the disciples scattered in fear and disappointment, in the case of Peter even denying that he had known Jesus. The story of Pentecost at the beginning of Acts shows Peter boldly proclaiming his faith in Jesus and calling others to "conversion" (Acts 2:38). What can we know about what happened in between?

In one sense what happened in between is completely unknown to us. We speak of the resurrection of Jesus, but the Gospel reports say nothing about the resurrection itself. No one witnessed it, and their reports begin after the event, either with stories about appearances of the already risen Jesus or about the empty tomb. About the resurrection itself they are completely silent, and in this sense we know nothing about the resurrection or what it was like.[4] In such a situation we are forced to use images and analogies, and the one which most readily suggests itself is that of someone coming back to consciousness out of coma or deep sleep. All analogies limp, and this one particularly so, for it suggests that Jesus came back

[4]See Willi Marxsen, *The Resurrection of Jesus of Nazareth* (Philadelphia: Fortress Press, 1970).

from the dead. It imagines resurrection after the analogy of the resuscitation or revivification of a corpse. But resurrection does not mean that Jesus "came back" from death, rather that he passed beyond death to a new life and a new existence. Of this passage and of this new life we have no direct knowledge, and therefore, like the Gospels, we must be silent. Even so-called "near death" experiences when people "come back" to life involve no such passage and are of no help.

Paul was once asked about these things in his controversy with the "spiritualists" in Corinth: "But, you may ask, how are the dead raised? In what kind of body? What a senseless question!" (1 Cor 15:35). Paul points to the variety of "bodies" in our experience, for example, the difference between that of a seed when it is sown and that of the fully grown plant. Even greater is the difference between our earthly bodies and a risen body. He can only speak of a risen body in imagined contrast to the earthly body we now possess:

> So it is with the resurrection of the dead. What is sown in the earth as a perishable thing is raised imperishable. Sown in humiliation, it is raised in glory; sown in weakness, it is raised in power; sown as an animal body, it is raised as a spiritual body (1 Cor 15:42-44).

He stresses both the continuity and discontinuity between these two stages of existence. It is the same body in both, but now totally transformed. Hence it is really the same Jesus of Nazareth who has been raised from the dead, but raised into a totally new mode of existence.

Paul's contrast at least helps us to know what the resurrection and risen body of Jesus are not. The resurrection is not a historical event either in the sense that it is accessible to historical, empirical investigation, nor in the sense that it was the reincorporation of Jesus back into the spatial, temporal existence of history. Resurrection is not a coming back into history but a passing beyond history.[5] It is more accurately called an eschatological event, which once again we know only in contrast to historical events. The eschaton is not a homogeneous continuation of history, but the consummation and fulfillment of history in a state of existence beyond time. Likewise the risen body of Jesus, says Paul, is not a physical

[5]See Wolfhart Pannenberg's treatment of the resurrection in *Jesus God and Man* (Philadelphia: Westminster Press, 1968) 53–114.

or "animal" body, but a "spiritual" body about which we can only say what it is not.

Although the New Testament is entirely silent about the resurrection event itself, it does speak of occurrences after the event. There are stories about finding the tomb of Jesus empty, and New Testament scholars are divided about whether to interpret them as rather late legendary material with an obvious apologetic purpose, or whether they have a historical basis. The two independent traditions in Mark and John would be evidence for the second position. But both sides are agreed that an empty tomb does not "prove" the resurrection, since that could be accounted for in any number of ways.[6] But stories about Jesus appearing to his disciples are part of the very earliest traditions and the very earliest form of the kerygma that Jesus is risen. What were the appearances of Jesus like?

New Testament scholars are agreed that the earliest written form of the resurrection kerygma appears in Paul's First Letter to the Corinthians. Just as in Paul's version of the Last Supper which we considered earlier, he says here that he is handing on a piece of the tradition which he has himself received:

> First and foremost, I handed on to you the facts which had been imparted to me: that Christ died for our sins, in accordance with the scriptures; that he was buried; that he was raised to life on the third day, according to the scriptures; that he appeared to Cephas, and afterwards to the twelve. Then he appeared to over five hundred of our brothers at once, most of whom are still alive, though some have died. Then he appeared to James, and afterwards to all the apostles. In the end he appeared even to me (1 Cor 15:3-8).

Since this letter was written in the early 50s, and speaks of a tradition Paul had already given to the Corinthians when he first visited them in the late 40s, a tradition which he had himself received earlier than that, the tradition takes us back at least to the middle 40s and to within ten to fifteen years of the events about which it speaks.

Reginald Fuller makes two observations about Paul's account of these events which perhaps throw light on the nature of Jesus'

---

[6]See Benedict Viviano, "The Gospel According to Matthew." *NJBC,* 673; and John Meier, "Jesus," *NJBC,* 1328. See also Raymond Brown, *The Virginal Conception and Bodily Resurrection of Jesus* (New York: Paulist Press, 1973).

appearances.[7] First, the Greek verb translated "he appeared" is *ophthe,* a verb used in both the Old and New Testaments to designate a revelatory encounter of some kind. It is used, for example, in the account of the angel of the Lord appearing to Moses in the burning bush (Exod 3:2), and again when Stephen tells the story of this in Acts (7:30). The verb emphasizes not the seeing or subjective experience of the recipient, but the revelatory initiative of the one appearing. Second, says Fuller, Paul lists all the appearances from the one to Cephas to the one to himself using identically the same word and format, suggesting that he understands all the appearances to have been of the same nature. If this is so, it is an important clue to how Paul understands all the appearances, for he speaks several times and in some detail of Jesus' appearance to himself.

Acts tells the story of Paul, while still a Pharisee, journeying from Jerusalem to Damascus with letters authorizing him to arrest any members of the synagogues there who were believers in Jesus. While on the way, "Suddenly a light flashed from the sky all around him." He fell to the ground and heard a voice saying: "Saul, Saul, why do you persecute me?" When he asked who was speaking to him, the voice replied: "I am Jesus whom you are persecuting." He was then told to continue on to Damascus and he would be told what to do. When he opened his eyes he discovered that he had been blinded by the light, so his companions, "who heard the voice but could see no one," led him into the city. There he met the disciple Ananias who restored his sight, and after being "filled with the Holy Spirit," he was converted and baptized (Acts 9:1-19). Paul's vision confirms the usual revelatory meaning of the verb for "he appeared," and if Jesus' other appearances were similar, they would all have had the nature of a revelatory encounter with Jesus of some kind. Moreover, the fact that only believers "saw" the risen Jesus indicates that the seeing involved was not seeing in the usual sense, but a seeing that involved the eyes of faith.

The Gospel stories of Jesus' appearances, while based on oral traditions which are earlier than Paul's First Letter to the Corinthians, were written down in their present form much later. The very "physical" details which are included in the stories could well

---

[7]Reginald Fuller, *The Formation of the Resurrection Narratives* (2nd ed., London: SPCK, 1980) 27–49.

represent a "physicalizing process" which accompanied the handing on of the stories. Such a process would have been the best literary way of expressing how real the experience of Jesus was, for we have no other way of speaking of spiritual realities except through physical metaphors. The telling and retelling of the stories also included their embellishment and adaptation to the various theological and apologetical purposes of the final editors of the Gospels.

But even the stories themselves in all their physical details portray the appearance of the risen Jesus as very different from the earthly Jesus they had known, and often "recognition" comes late in the story. This was the case with the two disciples on the way to Emmaus (Luke 24:13-32), with Mary of Magdala at the tomb (John 20:10-18), and with the disciples at the sea of Tiberias (John 21:1-14). However the development of the stories is interpreted, according to Paul the risen body of Jesus was not "physical" but "spiritual," and for him and the other disciples this did not lessen the reality of Jesus' presence nor his identity with the historical Jesus of Nazareth. We can speak, then, of the appearances as historical and as occurring in the real historical experience of the disciples. Indeed, it was the reality of the experience of the risen Jesus that gave the disciples the conviction to proclaim his death in faith and hope "until he comes."

This "until" shows, moreover, that, just as the resurrection must be understood together with its past in the life and death of Jesus as a single mystery, so too must it be understood in relation to its future. For resurrection is but the "firstfruits" of the harvest of the kingdom and the prelude to his second coming. Jesus began his public life proclaiming that the kingdom was at hand and ended it by giving his life on the cross for its coming. The experience of the risen Jesus was a pledge and a foretaste of this future coming that was still outstanding. Convinced by this experience that God was present and active in the history of Jesus just as he had been present and active in the history of the Exodus, the celebration of the paschal mystery in the Lord's Supper replaced the Passover celebration among the early Christians. Their celebration not only looked to the past in its commemoration of his death and to the present in its celebration of his risen presence, but also to the future in hope and anticipation of his second coming.

But as Jesus had taught his disciples on more than one occasion, hope did not consist in a passive waiting for his return, but was an active following. After he had spoken to them about his own approaching passion and death, he continued on the theme of discipleship:

> Then he called the people to him, as well as his disciples, and said to them: "Anyone who wishes to be a follower of mine must leave self behind; he must take up his cross and follow me" (Mark 8:34).

Likewise, after he had washed the disciples' feet at the Last Supper, he told them that a servant is not greater than his master. "I have set you an example: you are to do as I have done to you." Then he added: "If you know this, happy are you if you do it" (John 13:15, 17). Both the Synoptic and the Johannine texts indicate that discipleship is primarily a praxis and a doing the truth. This is the following that Paul alludes to when he speaks of "making up what is wanting in the sufferings of Christ" (Col 1:24), and says that we share his sufferings now "in order to share his glory hereafter" (Rom 8:17).

Before becoming theoretical statements about Jesus, then, faith is the practical process of following him. The fundamental challenge of Christian faith is not a *sacrificium intellectus,* but sharing in the *sacrificium crucis.* But this following of Jesus and association with him brings its own kind of knowledge, a knowledge through "connaturality" gained through shared life. Such knowledge creates union and fellowship with him and among the members of the community of faith. It is this fellowship which comes to expression in the ongoing celebration of the Lord's Supper. Insofar as the community is following in his footsteps and doing the truth that he did, the symbols of bread and wine which point in the first instance to the life and death of Jesus also become symbols of the community's living and dying with him. Without this communion with him in the real life of discipleship, the ritual celebration of the communion meal becomes a ritualism empty of real history.

But when the ritual communion meal is rooted in and gives expression to the real communion of discipleship, then the celebration of the Lord's Supper retains its roots in history. It is as closely related to the history of the present as Jesus' words and actions at the Last Supper were related to the historical events of his life and death. The bread and wine, which proclaim his death because he made them real symbols by his death on the cross, must also be real symbols of the cross of discipleship in the present, and

thereby real symbols of union and communion with him. Other-
wise, the servant is no longer like the master, and ritual has replaced
life and history as the locus of God's presence and activity in the
world and the locus of real union with Jesus.

But if resurrection signals the dawning of a new age for all of
humankind of which it is the firstfruits, and not in the first instance
the beginning of a new religion with new ritual and cultic activity,
the ritual and cultic activity must be in function and service of this
new age. It is for the sake of the ongoing transformation of the
present that his death must be proclaimed in ritual and shared in
history until he comes.

# 4

# A Theology of the Life of Jesus

Each of the four Gospels presents its own theological portrait of Jesus, its own theological interpretation of his life and death, but in moving from the three Synoptic Gospels to the Gospel of John a discernible theological shift takes place which has been variously described. Bultmann's observation that after the resurrection "the proclaimer became the proclaimed" is most evident in John, where the Jesus of the Synoptics who proclaimed the closeness of God's kingdom becomes himself a more explicit object of proclamation. For example, Jesus speaks little of himself in the Synoptic Gospels, but John contains numerous "I" sayings which portray Jesus asserting many things about himself. It is only John's Gospel which in its prologue speaks of Jesus as the Word of God become flesh, and hence only John speaks of an "incarnation." This has led to the distinction between John's "descending Christology" and the Synoptic accounts of Jesus "ascending" to the Father through his life, death, and resurrection. John's fuller attention to Jesus' identity has led to the further distinction between his so-called "high Christology" and the supposedly "low Christology" of the Synoptics, the terms indicating later and earlier stages in the development of Christology.

The manifest differences which characterize the New Testament interpretations of Jesus are also characteristic of the ongoing interpretation of the New Testament itself in subsequent centuries. In ancient times there were different "schools" of interpretation, the most famous among them being the schools at Antioch and Alexandria. Antioch, inspired more by the philosophy of Aristotle, placed more emphasis on the literal and historical meaning of texts, whereas Alexandria with its Platonic background looked more for the spiritual or allegorical meaning. Antioch tended to see more importance in the human and historical details of Jesus' life, while in Alexandria it was not the historical "letter," but the "spirit" of the text that was the primary concern. It is not surprising that these different approaches to Scripture, when combined with the different portraits of Jesus in Scripture to begin with, gave rise to different tendencies in the early Church's interpretation of the identity of Jesus. Each had its measure of truth and each could point to Scripture texts that supported it.

It was only when these tendencies were taken to an extreme and emphasized one aspect of the scriptural witness to the exclusion of other aspects that the Church had to make doctrinal decisions setting the limits of orthodox discussion. The first such decision was made at the Council of Nicaea in 325 against the position known as Arianism. This maintained that the Logos who became flesh in Jesus could not have been of one nature or substance or being with God because God was one and undivided. The Logos, therefore, had to be part of creation, the highest creature, to be sure, but not sharing in God's eternal nature. Arius was correct in stressing the oneness of God, but wrong in thinking that this excluded the possibility of differentiation within God and the ensuing possibility that God could freely enter into union with his creation. The decision of Nicaea that the Logos who became flesh in Jesus was of one being with God, that he was "begotten, not made," affirmed that such a union with creation was not only possible, but had become actual in Jesus.

Not everyone interpreted Nicaea in this way, however, for some did not see the reality of Jesus as truly human and a part of created reality. Jesus, they said, did indeed have a divine nature as Nicaea affirmed, but he had only this one nature, and hence their name, the Monophysites. Against this position the Council of Chalcedon in 451 affirmed that Jesus had both a divine and a human nature, that he was truly God and truly man, that in him God and creation truly become one. To assure this union it affirmed further that the two natures were united in the unity of a single person. This was said against a position associated with Nestorius which seemed to divide Jesus into two persons. Chalcedon's concern was to assure fidelity to the entire scriptural witness about Jesus and to prevent one-sided interpretations that made a partial truth the whole truth. In Jesus there was a true union between the divine and the human, and one side of this union could not be maintained at the expense of or by watering down the other.

Despite the differences among these three unorthodox readings of Scripture, namely, that Jesus was human, but only human, or that he was divine, but only divine, or that the human and the divine were not united in a single person, they all have one thing in common which is the real crux of the matter. They all denied the possibility of a genuine unity between God and created human reality. They maintained that if Jesus was human he could not also be divine, or if he was divine he could not also be human, or if he was both the two could not really be united in one person. The fruit of the decisions of the early councils was the affirmation that in Jesus, God, while remaining truly God, has really entered into the world and into history, has truly "become flesh," and that therefore, at least since Jesus, God and the world, though never identical, are also never separate.

What characterized the efforts of these early Church councils to remain faithful to the entire scriptural witness to Jesus was that this fidelity did not take the form of merely repeating scriptural formula. Rather, since they had to address questions which had not arisen in New Testament times, they interpreted the scriptural accounts of Jesus in concepts and language that were drawn from their own cultural situation and were able to speak to their own cultural situation. They were inculturating the faith in their own time and place, and had to do so if the faith was to remain alive. In doing this they were doing what Scripture itself had done, for the various theological portraits of Jesus in the New Testament can be explained at least in part as adapting the one faith in Jesus to the cultural and religious situations of different Christian communities, for example, the Jewish and the Gentile communities. For both the New Testament and the early Church councils, then, fidelity to the past did not mean repeating the formulas of the past, but discovering the language which could express the same faith in an ever new present. Mere repetition of the language of the past could impede rather than facilitate the communication of the faith in the present. To say the same thing to a new audience living in a new cultural situation they had to say something different.

In the light of this historical process, it is clear why Anselm of Canterbury could speak of theology as "faith seeking understanding," seeking an understanding and an expression that will keep the faith alive in a new cultural context. His elaboration of the theory of satisfaction which we considered in the last chapter is an excellent example of faith seeking an understanding of Jesus' life and death for his own time. He understood both his Christian tradition and his own feudal times deeply enough to see how the former could make sense and be inculturated in his own day. Theology in Anselm's sense is an ongoing process that must keep one eye on the past of Christian tradition and the other on the present. It must be in touch both with the past and with the present in order to keep the two in touch with each other. For Christian faith is about God and history, the history not only of the past, but of the present and the future as well. A faith that was in touch only with God's action in the past would be the faith of a museum rather than of a living God and a living Christian community.

For this reason faith in every age is always a *search* for God rather than a possession. For the truth of God is contained not in books, but in the divine presence in the ongoing history of Jesus to which the books give witness. The history of God may be said to be unfinished and incomplete until God "comes again" in the consummation of history at the end of time. Hence this presence is not only in word or in ritual which recall the past, but also in the history of the present to which word and ritual also point. In the light of and guided by God's presence in Jesus in the past, faith seeks to discover God's ongoing presence in the unfinished history of Jesus today. The search for an "understanding of faith" of which Anselm speaks is not merely for a more subtle theoretical understanding of truths past, but the discovery of the reality and meaning of this truth as an event in the present. The question of Jesus' identity, then, the Christological question, is a question about both the past and the present. What was it about Jesus that led to his identification as the event of God's own truth and Word becoming flesh in history, and how does this truth and this Word continue to be embodied in the flesh of his ongoing history in the present?

Posed in this way the Christological question about Jesus' identity is seen in a different light than it was seen in the early Church councils. Since Christian faith is not about God's abstract divine nature as known through philosophical speculation, but about God's free self-revelation in history, its notion of God is derived not from philosophy but from God's action in history. The Christian faith's fundamental knowledge of God is not what God has to be as divine nature, but who God has freely chosen to be in sovereign freedom. The God who is known from God's free presence in history is, nevertheless, God in God's real self, for it is God as God has freely chosen to be and to be revealed. Moreover, Christian faith finds this revelation especially in the history of Jesus of Nazareth. It does not begin with an abstract notion of divine nature which it then affirms of Jesus, but discovers who God is in Jesus. The shift in the focus of the Christological question about the identity of Jesus, then, is from the abstract nature of God to concrete history. In this light Christology becomes a theology of the life and history of Jesus.

But to be faithful to Nicaea and Chalcedon it must be a genuine *theology* of his life; that is, it must discover why this man who was fully human, as Chalcedon taught, was truly the incarnation of divine life, truly "one in being with the Father" as the creed of Nicaea-Constantinople says. It must see in the life and person of Jesus the same kind of differentiated unity between Jesus and God which Chalcedon expressed from its point of view in the terminology of "two natures" and "one person." It will begin with history and the human Jesus, because it is in the human flesh that the Word of God became that God revealed himself and can be known. It will focus precisely on the life of Jesus, because it was in the history of his freedom that Jesus achieved his human identity and therein revealed his divine identity, indeed, revealed what divine identity means. A theology of the life of Jesus, then, finds its starting point for speaking of the divinity of Jesus precisely in his humanity, not above it or alongside it, for it is in human flesh and history that the Word of God has become incarnate. It asks what it was about this human life that brought those who witnessed it to see Jesus as the incarnation of God's life and presence.

We have already discussed the human identity of Jesus in the light of his symbolic words and gestures at the Last Supper. There he spoke of himself and his self-understanding when he said that the symbols of bread and wine were his Body and Blood, were himself. To identify himself he did not use any of the religious titles of his Jewish religion, nor the concepts of Greek philosophy, but the very simple human realities of bread and wine. This is what he claimed to be, and his actions the following day made his claim true. In John's Gospel Jesus made a similar claim when he washed the disciples' feet, namely, that he was servant. This claim too he fulfilled the following day. If both of these symbols express the meaning of the life and death of Jesus as he himself interpreted it, our question above becomes more specific. Why do these real symbols of the human love of Jesus reveal the incarnation of God's presence in this human love, the very Word of God become flesh?

The answer to this question presupposes some particular content and meaning of the word "God," a meaning revealed in the life and death of Jesus. John offers a theological reflection which shows that the Last Supper symbols are not only symbols of Jesus' humanity, but also of his divinity. The reflection occurs in the midst of an exhortation to his brothers and sisters to love one another. The exhortation echoes the "one commandment" that Jesus gave to his disciples in his farewell discourse that they "love one another," and his words that it was "by this that everyone shall know that you are my disciples." John asks why this should be so and offers the following reflection:

> Beloved, let us love one another, because love is from God. Everyone who loves is born of God and knows God. He who does not love does not know God. For God is love. And his love was revealed to us in this, that he sent his only Son into the world to bring us life. . . . Though God has never been seen by anyone, God himself dwells in us if we love one another; his love is brought to perfection in us (1 John 4:7-12).

John's logic is very simple. One must love because to live such a life is to be born of God and love brings knowledge of God. This is so because God is love.

The knowledge of God that John speaks of here is not a theoretical knowledge nor knowing God as an object of knowledge, for he says that no one has ever seen God. It is not a knowledge which comes from without, but from within the experience of loving one's neighbor. Existing in this kind of relationship brings knowledge of God because God exists in this kind of relationship. It is a knowledge which comes by actually sharing God's life, by "being born of God," and hence it is a knowledge of God by "connaturality." The prologue to John's Gospel speaks in a similar vein when it says of those who accepted Jesus and gave him their allegiance that "he gave them the right to become children of God," not born of any human stock, "but the offspring of God himself" (John 1:12-13). The life of God that they share brings them an experiential and existential knowledge of God. For "no one has ever seen God," but God's only Son "has made him known" (John 1:18).

If one asks from this Johannine perspective and this understanding of God what it was in the human life and death of Jesus that led John to see Jesus as the Word made flesh, it was the quality of his love. God is love, and therefore human love is the incarnation and revelation of God. Where this love is most fully present, there is God most fully present and revealed. It was the love of Jesus that revealed the nature of God and "made him known." Hence John's narrative of the passion as the story of Jesus' love and his portrait of Jesus' death as his loving "unto the end" are not only the story of his humanity, but also the revelation of his divinity in his humanity. In Jesus the eternal life and being of the Son became flesh because the eternal love of the Son for the Father became flesh in Jesus' human life and death as God's human son. The eternal relationship of the Son to the Father was lived out in flesh and history in the relationship of Jesus to the Father.

From John's perspective it is also clear that the more fully human Jesus was, the more real his human love was, the more truly could he be "God's only Son." The humanity and divinity of Jesus do not vary in inverse proportion, the more of the one the less of the other, but rather in direct proportion. One need not think of the humanity of Jesus as something alien to his divinity, but rather should think of his humanity as the flesh which was created precisely for the purpose of being the incarnation of divine life.[1] As the early councils taught, there is a real difference between "human nature" and "divine nature," between what each is in and of itself. God could have existed in God's eternal nature without creation and without incarnation. But in the sovereign freedom of grace God created human nature, and indeed created it to be the embodiment and incarnation of divine life.

---

[1] See Karl Rahner, "On the Theology of the Incarnation," *Theological Investigations* 4 (New York and London, 1966) 115-117.

In the actual order of creation, then, when the "Word became flesh," the eternal Son as he is in his own divine nature "became" identical with the person of Jesus, whose human nature is the expression, the human form and human face of his divine nature. The difference between the two is not the difference between two "things" juxtaposed, as though Jesus could use one or the other of his natures at will. The difference is rather the differentiated unity of God's Word and its human expression.[2] The Son of God is forever united with flesh and with history because, since the incarnation, the Son in his "pure" divine nature is but an abstract possibility that could have been, but which has now been outstripped in the history of God's freedom and love.

It is also important to note that what is the literary prologue to John's Gospel is theologically its epilogue. In order for the Son of God to become flesh in Jesus, Jesus also had to become the Son of God by living out his life of sonship in freedom. This is why the Christological question about Jesus' identity must be answered in a theology of the *life* of Jesus, for it was throughout his entire life that the eternal relationship of the Son to the Father became flesh. The incarnation was not an instantaneous event at the beginning of Jesus' existence, but the lifelong process of his being and becoming God's Son. Were this not the case, were Jesus merely a human puppet on a divine string, or merely the human "instrument" of a divine person within, he would not have been free and would not have been human as the Council of Chalcedon taught. If Jesus could not have said "no" to his call and his mission, his "yes" would have been stripped of any human value and meaning. Jesus' living and dying as God's son was not only the revelation, but also the realization of his sonship. It was only after Jesus had freely lived out a life of sonship by loving "unto the end" that John could say in his theological reflection upon, and his epilogue to, this life that in him the Word and Son became flesh.

There is no opposition, then, between the "descending" Christology of John's prologue and the more "ascending" Christology of the Synoptic Gospels. They are both necessary and complementary moments in the coming to be of God's relationship to the world and to history. It is a personal relationship which there-

---

[2]Karl Rahner, "The Theology of the Symbol," *op. cit.*, 221–252, especially 235–240 on the Logos as symbol.

fore requires freedom on both sides. Descending Christology is an image for God's call and offer of sonship; ascending Christology is an image for the free response of Jesus that he made throughout his life. The ensuing union and relationship required both God's "yes" and the free "yes" of Jesus in response. Since the initiative must be on God's part, descending Christology is the condition which makes ascending Christology possible, while Jesus' response is what makes this possibility a real and actual historical event.

When the freedom of Jesus is understood in a genuinely human way as the process of creating his identity out of the possibilities offered him by his Father, the traditional notion of the "sinlessness" of Jesus must not be understood in a way that makes him less free than other human beings. The notion that Jesus could not or did not sin cannot mean that this did not lie within the possibilities of his freedom. The prayer of Jesus in the garden of Gethsemane that the Father "take this cup away from me" (Mark 14:36) shows clearly enough that the fidelity and obedience of Jesus were not the automatic response of someone with no other choice. But his "Not what I will, but what thou wilt" that follows shows that his love was such that he remained faithful to his Father despite the struggle. Such love does not make Jesus less free but more free than other human beings, for he had the freedom to remain faithful to what he had freely chosen to be and to do.

Like the freedom of Jesus, so too must his knowledge be understood in a genuinely human way as something that he acquired in the course of his life by learning and experience. This is true also of his own self-understanding. Thinking of Jesus as having "two natures" side by side can give the impression that he had access to a divine intellect that he could consult at will. Such an image supposes that the divine nature of the Logos did not quite become flesh, did not really enter into the finiteness and limits of human existence. It also belies the witness of the New Testament which portrays Jesus as learning gradually and being surprised and ignorant of certain things and supports the testimony that "he was like us in all things but sin" (Heb 4:15). Jesus had to discover who he was and what his mission entailed as his life unfolded and as he confronted the opportunities and challenges that faced him. Since we do not have a biography or history of Jesus in the modern sense, we have no way of being sure what in the Gospel accounts represents Jesus' own self-understanding, and what is rather an interpretation of him by the early Christian communities in the light of their experience of the risen Jesus.

This is especially true of the many titles applied to Jesus and the supposed "claims" about himself implied by these titles which were verified in the resurrection. But we do not have to understand the resurrection as the extrinsic confirmation or verification of explicit claims made by Jesus during his earthly life. If his life and death were the total self-emptying and self-abandonment in faith, hope, and love that the Gospels portray, including the abandonment of any kind of expectations and claims except that of being bread broken and wine poured out, then the resurrection should rather be understood as the fullness of life that is the intrinsic fruit of such self-emptying.

Jesus' knowledge of God and of his own relationship to God would then be understood in the sense in which we have already seen John speak of knowing God. Living a life of love, according to John, *is* living God's life. In this very doing and being God is known by sharing his being. In Jesus' perfect love he was "one in being with the Father" and therein would have known God by connaturality. His union in being was his union in knowledge. How Jesus may or may not have objectified this into concepts or titles is of secondary importance, and in any case very difficult for us to know given the nature of the New Testament literature.

In using the same analogy of knowledge to understand Jesus' knowledge of God and the knowledge had by anyone who loves (the analogy drawn from the sense of touch and being "in touch" with a reality rather than "seeing" a reality as an object), the distinction between Jesus' knowledge of God and that of his brothers and sisters is not thereby blurred. John presents Jesus as the source of this knowledge for others, as the one who "has made him known" and revealed him to others (John 1:18). His was the fullness of knowledge because of the fullness of his union, while that of others is partial in both respects. Just as when Jesus is called the "firstborn of many brothers and sisters" (Rom 8:29) and his resurrection the "firstfruits" (1 Cor 15:23), this "first" is not merely the first of a series, but first in the sense of a principle and source. Jesus, then, is forever the giver and the revealer, and those "who have received him and yielded him their allegiance" are forever recipients of the "grace and truth [which] came through Jesus Christ" (John 1:12, 17).

When a theology of the life of Jesus looks to John's understanding of God to find the properly theological element in Jesus' identity, that which makes him "one in being with the Father," it is the love of Jesus which is the identifying element. God's power was present and manifest in the power of Jesus' love. That power continues to be present in his ongoing history, and John speaks of this continuation as the "sending of the Spirit."

# 5

# The Sending of the Spirit

The relationship of Jesus in his particular historical moment to the larger and universal history of which he is a part comes to expression in the New Testament as the relationship between Jesus and the "Spirit." Just as the Gospel witness to Jesus includes a variety of theological portraits, so too is the Spirit spoken of in many and various images. The Spirit both precedes Jesus in God's historical action in the world and follows him as someone whom he "sends." Seeing the Last Supper symbols as one theological interpretation of the life of Jesus, expressing both the human and divine content of his life, death, and resurrection, how do these symbols point also to his Spirit as the larger historical context and content within which he must be understood? Since John speaks of the relationship of Jesus and the Spirit in his account of Jesus' "farewell discourses" to the disciples at the Last Supper, we shall begin by looking at how he describes this relationship.

At first sight there is some ambiguity in John's description. Jesus begins by promising "another" who will be with his disciples after he leaves: "I will ask the Father, and he will give you another to be your Advocate, who will be with you forever, even the Spirit of truth" (John 14:16). As Jesus describes this other Advocate, he seems, on the one hand, to represent something of a complement or an addition to the truth which Jesus himself both taught and was in his historical life and death:

> I have yet many things to say to you, but you cannot hear them now. When the Spirit of truth comes, he will guide you into all truth (John 16:12-13).

On the other hand, however, the Spirit's teaching is not something different from that of Jesus, but a "reminder" of what Jesus taught:

> These things I have spoken to you while I am still with you. But the Advocate, the Holy Spirit, whom the Father will send in my name, he will teach you all things, and remind you of all that I have said to you (John 14:25-26).

This same point is made when Jesus says that when the Spirit comes, "he will bear witness to me" (John 15:26). Finally, Jesus makes the enigmatic remark: "If I do not go away, the Advocate will not come to you. But if I go, I will send him to you" (John 16:7).

Beginning with this last point, why is it that Jesus must leave if the Spirit is to come? Jesus' "departure" is his giving his life for them on the cross, the final and fullest act of his love. Only when he does this do they receive his Spirit. John makes this point in a variety of ways. Jesus said that he "must be lifted up" so that everyone who has faith in him may have eternal life (John 3:14-15), and that when he is "lifted up from the earth" he will draw men to himself. He said this, John adds, to indicate "the kind of death he was to die" (John 12:32). Likewise, it is only when the grain of wheat falls into the ground and dies that it "bears much fruit" (John 12:24). The "must" of Jesus' having to "leave" and having to be "lifted up" and having to "fall into the ground and die" all point to the same necessity: it was only Jesus' loving "unto the end" that proved effective in the lives of his disciples. Only love can beget love and new life in others. If the meaning of Jesus' Cross and resurrection is that his giving of his life for others was for him passage into new life, the sending of the Spirit means further that only such love can beget new life in others. He had to leave or his Spirit could not come.

This throws light on the other texts in which John speaks of the relationship of Jesus and the Spirit. "The Spirit of truth," says Jesus, "will guide you into all truth," but this is not a truth other than or in addition to the truth that Jesus taught and did. For it is to Jesus that the Spirit is "to bear witness," and it is of what Jesus told the disciples that the Spirit is to "remind" them. The Spirit is required not because something is wanting on the part of Jesus but rather on the part of the disciples. The Spirit must open their eyes and ears to the truth. He is the interior principle by which they are transformed and brought to a *realization* of the truth, to what John calls "faith" in him. Such faith requires what in later theology is called grace. The disciples could not simply decide to believe. This grace is God's self-communication, and for John this means the communication of God's love. This is the truth Jesus communicated to them by doing the truth on the cross, and this is the truth that made them free to believe. The Spirit of truth is the Spirit of love, and this is the "grace and truth [which] came through Jesus Christ" (John 1:17).

John portrays in telling imagery the moment when this promise to send the Spirit was fulfilled, which was for the disciples the moment of recognition and realization. When Jesus appeared to the disciples locked behind closed doors in fear on the Sunday evening after his death, "he breathed on them, saying, 'Receive the Holy Spirit!' " (John 20:22). Breath is the principle of life, and breathing on them is the bestowal of the same principle of life and the same Spirit that animated him. The image would have had a familiar ring to John's readers, for they had read in the Scriptures: "In the beginning when God created the heavens and earth" the *ruah* of God, God's breath or Spirit, hovered over the waters of chaos and darkness (Gen 1:1-2), and that when God created Adam he "breathed into his nostrils the breath of life" (Gen 2:7). To them the image signaled that now Jesus was inaugurating the new creation and the new age by breathing new life and a new Spirit upon his disciples.

The image also recalls Jesus' words to Nicodemus early in John's Gospel. When Nicodemus came to Jesus by night and said that Jesus must be a teacher come from God because of the signs that accompanied his teaching, Jesus replied in very oblique fashion: "In truth, in very truth I tell you, unless one is born anew he cannot see the kingdom of God." Nicodemus took Jesus' words literally and was understandably confused, so he asked how someone can enter into his mother's womb and be born anew. Jesus explained: "No one can enter the kingdom of God unless he is born of water and the Spirit." Nicodemus was still puzzled, and as the conversation continued, Jesus said:

> This Son of Man must be lifted up as the serpent was lifted up by Moses in the wilderness, so that everyone who has faith in him may in him possess eternal life (John 3:14-15).

The allusion to Moses and the serpent refers to the incident during the journey to the Promised Land when the people complained of their difficult conditions in the desert and were set upon by poisonous serpents. At the Lord's instruction Moses erected a bronze serpent as a standard, and anyone who looked upon it was healed of the serpent's bite (Num 21:4-9). So too Jesus had to be "lifted up" to be the source of healing and new life. When, then, Jesus countered Nicodemus' reference to his signs with an oblique allusion to his being lifted up and the need to be born anew, he was saying that it was not the signs that he performed that would enable Nicodemus to see, but the sign that he *was,* namely, the sign of the Cross which was the sign of his love. This was the source of the Spirit who brought faith and thereby birth into new and eternal life.

As we have seen, Jesus speaks twice in John's Gospel of being "lifted up," saying on one occasion that it would "draw" people to him, and on the other that it would bring them to faith in him. Seeing the two texts together throws light on how John understands "faith" in Jesus. In the Nicodemus story it is clear that such faith is not a "conclusion" one draws from signs or marvels that Jesus performs, for he must be lifted up in order that people might have faith in him. Faith follows rather from "being drawn" to Jesus, and he says that it is only by being lifted up on the cross in the final and fullest act of his love that he would draw people to himself. Faith is not "grasping" something about Jesus, but "being grasped" by him. The better analogy for the kind of knowing that faith involves is not drawn from the sense of sight but from the sense of touch. Faith is "being touched" and "being affected" by Jesus, and only by being drawn in this way is one empowered to see. The blindness of which John's Gospel speaks is not cured by argument but by encounter with the Cross. By being lifted up on the cross in love, Jesus lifted the disciples out of themselves and empowered them to love. He had to be lifted up if they were to receive his Spirit.

This also throws light on what Jesus means by "example" when he says after washing the disciples' feet at the Last Supper: "I have set you an example: you are to do as I have done for you" (John 13:15). His "example" is not merely an external norm for the disciples to see or a word to be understood and followed, but one which has to touch, affect, and "draw" them. For the footwashing points to his being lifted up on the cross where he becomes servant in the fullest sense and "unto the end." It was when he did this truth, when his Word became flesh on the cross, that he became a powerful and empowering example, powerful enough to "draw" the disciples to himself and to faith. Jesus had no power on the cross but the power of his love; this was the only power that could transform them, give them new life in his Spirit, and make them free to follow his example. Jesus revealed who he was and brought the disciples to faith not by the power of argument, but by the power of his example and the power of his love.

It was only against the background of his example and by the power of his Spirit that the disciples were able to see and recognize the risen Jesus in faith. Hence the Spirit had to "bear witness" to Jesus and "remind" them of Jesus. Just as for Jesus the path to the resurrection lies through the Cross, so too for the disciples the path to seeing the risen Jesus in faith lies through the power of the Cross. They had to be touched and transformed by it before they could see. Just as the psalmist said, "Taste, then, and see, that the Lord is good" (Ps 34:8), so too does seeing the risen Jesus require that one has tasted and been touched by the "goodness" of Jesus.

We speak of the "eyes of faith," but all of the senses, tasting, hearing, and touching as well as seeing, provide us with analogies for understanding the kind of knowledge involved in faith. It is not just a seeing but also a tasting and touching, a being touched and being drawn. For John faith is not just a new way of seeing but also a new way of being, a new life. It is not just a transformation of one's knowledge, but also and primarily a transformation of one's self. In John the Spirit is the interior principle by which one is born anew and animated by this new life, the Spirit who is communicated by the power of Jesus' Cross.

Paul, too, often speaks of the Spirit in relationship to Jesus and as the interior and empowering principle of faith in Jesus. "No one can say, 'Jesus is Lord,' except by the Holy Spirit" (1 Cor 12:3). This confession of his Lordship is a confession of his resurrection when "he became the Son of God in power" (Rom 1:4). What we have spoken of above as the power of his Cross Paul here calls the power of his resurrection. But the two, Cross and resurrection together, form the single paschal mystery of Jesus, which is the empowering mystery of his love. When the resurrection is seen in relation to his Cross, the nature of his Lordship and power is the power of his love. When, conversely, the Cross is seen in relation to the resurrection, the resurrection is the expression of the new life that is the fruit of his love and self-emptying. Paul likewise says that it is the Spirit "who enables us to cry, 'Abba, Father.'" For "all who are moved by the Spirit of God are sons of God," and he makes them "children of God" and "fellow-heirs with Christ" (Rom 8:14-17). The Spirit who enables one to confess the sonship of Jesus also gives participation in that sonship. For the new life that the Spirit brings is the life of the Son, and faith in him is the process of assimilation into and association with his life.

Luke also sees the Spirit as an interior and empowering principle from his own theological perspective which he develops in the story of the Pentecost event at the beginning of Acts. He describes the disciples gathered together to celebrate the feast when suddenly they heard coming from the sky "a noise like that of a strong driving wind," and there came to rest on each of them "tongues like flames of fire" (Acts 2:1-3). The narrative details of the rushing wind and the fire are associated with theophanies in the Old Testament, and here they signal the coming of the Holy Spirit: "And they were all filled with the Holy Spirit and began to talk in other tongues, as the Spirit gave them power of utterance" (Acts 2:4). There is some ambiguity in the meaning "other tongues." Were they speaking in foreign languages, which is the impression Luke gives when he says that the multitude of Jews from many different nations whom they were addressing were bewildered because they all heard the apostles speaking in their own language and telling of the mighty works of God in their own tongue? Or does the phrase refer to glossolalia or speaking in tongues, that is, rapturous musical sounds like words, but without any particular meaning, to express enthusiasm or ecstasy, which would explain the other reaction Luke records, the mocking comment of the audience that they were drunk on new wine?

Whatever the correct interpretation, the sequel makes clear Luke's intention in telling the story. Peter stands with the other apostles to address the crowd and begins by quoting the prophet Joel:

> God says, "This will happen in the last days: I will pour out upon everyone a portion of my Spirit; and your sons and daughters shall

prophesy; your young men shall see visions, and your old men shall dream dreams. . ." (Acts 2:17).

Against the background of this prophecy of the end-time he then speaks of Jesus of Nazareth:

> Men of Israel, listen to me: I speak of Jesus of Nazareth, a man singled out by God and made known to you through miracles, portents and signs which God worked among you through him, as you well know. When he had been given up to you, by the deliberate will and plan of God, you used heathen men to crucify and kill him. But God raised him to life again, setting him free from the pangs of death, because it could not be that death should keep him in its grip. . . . The Jesus we speak of has been raised by God, as we can all bear witness. Exalted thus with God's right hand, he received the Holy Spirit from the Father, as was promised, and all that you now see and hear flows from him (Acts 2:22-24; 32-33).

In his last words to his disciples before his departure at the end of Luke's Gospel Jesus had promised to send the Spirit: "And mark this: I am sending upon you my Father's promised gift; so stay here in this city until you are armed with the power from above" (Luke 24:49). The version of this scene at the beginning of Acts elaborates further on the nature of this power: "But you will receive power when the Holy Spirit comes upon you; and you will bear witness for me in Jerusalem, and all over Judea and Samaria, and away to the ends of the earth" (Acts 1:8). The outpouring of the Spirit on Pentecost is the fulfillment of this promise and the bestowal of this power to give witness to Jesus.

The story of Pentecost portrays the Spirit not only as the source of new life for the disciples, but also of new power, the power to communicate this new life to others. The presence and activity of the Spirit whom Jesus sends signifies not only the emergence of the new community of believers who in Paul's analogy form a single body living by the same Spirit (1 Cor 12), it also signifies the beginning of the community's mission to others. Peter begins this mission immediately by addressing the crowd and telling them the good news of the resurrection of Jesus. God would pour out his Spirit not only on the first disciples, but also through them "on all flesh." When Peter finished his narrative of the crucifixion and resurrection of Jesus, the people "were cut to the heart," and he exhorts them to repentance: "Repent and be baptized, everyone of you, in the name of Jesus the Messiah for the forgiveness of your sins; and you will receive the gift of the Holy Spirit'' (Acts 2:37-38).

The good news that Peter has to preach is not just what happened to Jesus, that God raised him from the dead, but also what can happen to them: they can receive the gift of the Holy Spirit. In the context of John's and Paul's theology of the Spirit, the good news of the sending of the Spirit does not refer to something other than the good news of the resurrection, but broadens it to include the possibility of others sharing in his risen life. Just as Jesus died for others, so too was he raised from the dead for others, to share this life and this Spirit with others. The good news is the good news of sonship, the sonship of Jesus and the sonship of all who believe, for he is the ''firstfruits of those who have fallen asleep'' (1 Cor 15:20). It is into this life that they must be born anew of water and the Spirit in order to ''see'' and ''enter'' the kingdom. ''For the promise is to you and to your children and to all who are far off, everyone whom the Lord our God may call to him'' (Acts 2:39).

The similarity between Peter's exhortation to ''repent'' and Jesus' own call to ''repent and believe the good news'' at the beginning of his ministry is striking, but the similarity does not end there. Another aspect of the power of the Spirit becomes evident in the following chapter of Acts. Peter and John were on their way up to the Temple when they met a man who had been crippled from birth begging at the Temple gate. Though Peter had no money to give him, ''What I have,'' he said, ''I give you: in the name of Jesus Christ of Nazareth, walk'' (Acts 3:6). What he had was the Spirit of Jesus and the power of his Spirit to heal. Just as in the stories of Jesus' own healing, the cured man gave praise to God and all those who saw him walking ''were filled with wonder and amazement.'' Peter was empowered by the Spirit to give witness to Jesus not only in word, but also in deed. Through the sending of the Spirit Jesus' own history and ministry continue in the words and deeds which the disciples perform in his name.

To the disciples' apparent surprise and disappointment, however, this history was to continue beyond their own imminent expectations and into an indefinite future. ''Lord,'' they ask expectantly before Jesus has left them, ''is this the time when you are to restore the kingdom to Israel?'' (Acts 1:6). Jesus' answer avoids the question of dates and times which are hidden in the

Father's will, but assures them of the power of the Spirit who will remain with them. When he leaves, then, they are told not to stand "looking up into the sky" (Acts 1:11), but to return to Jerusalem for the tasks that lay ahead. Jesus' death and resurrection was but the beginning of the new and final age and the promise of its eventual consummation in the kingdom of God. In the meantime they were to live by this promise and give witness to him by the power of his Spirit until he comes again.

But the line which extends through the Spirit from Jerusalem through Judea and Samaria to the ends of the earth, and from the historical moment of Jesus until the end of time, also had its beginning through the Spirit before Jesus. What is to have its fulfillment in the second coming of Jesus also had its beginnings before his coming in time. The New Testament gives clear witness to this more universal aspect of the presence and activity of the Spirit. The God who in this final age "has spoken to us in the Son" has also in former times "spoken to our forefathers in fragmentary and varied fashion through the prophets" (Heb 1:1-2). If this text is not read in an exclusive sense, it does not exclude the possibility that this same God has spoken through others besides the Jewish prophets and spoken in other phases of history than the one of which Jesus is more immediately and directly a part. Indeed, if the God of Jesus and the prophets "wishes all men to be saved and to come to a knowledge of the truth" (1 Tim 2:4), then it is the Christian assumption and the Christian hope that God's Spirit has been present and active in the history of all peoples.

For the Judaeo-Christian tradition affirms that there is one God and creator of all people and one Lord of all history and that this single human history has a common origin and a common destiny. It is in the context of this larger history and longer time that Christian tradition sees Jesus as the "fullness of time," excluding no moment as part of this whole. As part of this single history, and indeed its fullness, Jesus is related to every other moment as every other moment is related to him. This mutual relationship can best be explained if the Spirit which he sent and which he himself received has been present from the beginning as God's immanent and abiding presence in his creation. The "breath" or "Spirit" of God that hovered over the waters of chaos "in the beginning when God created the heavens and the earth" has never been absent from creation. Not even the power of sin that entered into the world which was created good could vanquish this Spirit, for God's power, which is the power of love, is greater than the power of evil. If ever and whenever God's Spirit has been absent from the world, this would be so not because God has withdrawn, but because God has been rejected. But God's "yes" to creation has never ceased to be uttered even in the face of human "no." This is what endows the human "yes" of Jesus with its universal and salvific significance. It was the response that created union and reconciliation for this entire human history.

The Synoptic Gospels clearly portray this other dimension of Jesus' relationship to the Spirit, his receiving as well as sending the Spirit. Matthew and Luke place the conception of Jesus under the power of the Holy Spirit. In Luke's Annunciation scene, when Mary was troubled by the strange message of the angel of the Lord, the angel reassures her: "The Holy Spirit will come upon you, and the power of the Most High will overshadow you" (Luke 1:35). All three Synoptic Gospels portray Jesus as receiving the Holy Spirit on the occasion of his baptism by John in the Jordan. Mark, for example, describes Jesus coming up out of the water "and the Spirit, like a dove, descending upon him," a sign that he was God's beloved son upon whom God's favor rests (Mark 1:10). All three evangelists portray Jesus going out into the wilderness under the guidance of the Spirit to be tempted by Satan. The temptation scenes make clear that Jesus' acceptance of and response to the Spirit was not an automatic response, but the free and human response of Jesus who lived this response freely "unto the end." By doing so, through his Cross and resurrection he "became the Son of God in power" (Rom 1:4), and was able to "send" the Spirit that he had received.

It is this reciprocal relationship between Jesus and the Spirit that prevents the uniqueness of his particular person and his particular historical moment from becoming a divisive particularism or exclusivism. The universal activity of God's Spirit in the world and in history, the same Spirit whom Jesus himself received and gave to his disciples, associates all other moments of this history with Jesus and him with them. If, indeed, "there is no other name under heaven granted to men by which they can be saved" (Acts 4:12), the concrete content of the name of Jesus is the content he gave it through his life and death. This content is his love, and wherever love is present the name and the Spirit of Jesus are also present, whatever might be the variety of names it bears and forms it takes throughout historical times and cultures.[1] Only the absence of love, in whatever form and by whatever name this, too, appears, is the absence of the name of Jesus and the absence of the Spirit of Jesus.

The community that bears his name is by that very name related to the activity of his Spirit not only within but also beyond its own boundaries. It has its own distinctive identity as Jesus himself did, although its identity does not constitute a barrier, but a bond with those outside its community. It gives witness to God's universal call to grace. Its faith that the name of Jesus, that is, his particular historical moment, was the fullest historical embodiment and manifestation of God's presence, and its hope that this moment was the inauguration of a new age that will culminate in the coming of God's kingdom for all people, is not a triumphalistic theory or exclusive claim to superiority, but a practical imperative. It is the challenge to respond to the presence of the Spirit of Jesus wherever the Spirit is at work in Jesus' ongoing history in the present.

[1]Karl Rahner, who was one of the major voices in this century to affirm the universal presence of God's Spirit and the offer of his grace, speaks of its "anonymous" presence outside explicit Christianity. Among his many writings on this theme, see "Anonymous Christians," *Theological Investigations* 6 (London and New York, 1969) 390–398; and "Atheism and Implicit Christianity," *Theological Investigations* 9 (London and New York, 1972) 145–164.

# 6

# Kingdom to Church

The seriousness and even urgency with which the first disciples of Jesus accepted this challenge is evident in the New Testament accounts of their early activity. Their joy in the experience of the risen Jesus and of the power of his Spirit was not the complacent possession of a goal already attained but the joy of hope in one that lay ahead. As is the case with the life of Jesus, however, we do not have in the New Testament a history of the life and activity of the early disciples but rather a theological account of how they understood themselves in their new situation. This understanding, like their understanding of Jesus and the meaning of his resurrection, underwent change under the pressure of historical events. These changes would also affect their understanding of the Last Supper symbols through which we have interpreted the life, death, and resurrection of Jesus. In this process of change the symbols became less focused on the kingdom and more focused on the Church.

We examined these symbols against the background of the Jewish Passover meal and in the context of the kingdom which Jesus explicitly mentions in his words and actions interpreting his death: "I tell you this: never again shall I drink from the fruit of the vine until that day when I drink it new in the kingdom of God" (Mark 14:25). It is difficult if not impossible to know what Jesus' explicit intentions were with regard to the group of disciples gathered at the Supper with him and the larger group who had become his followers. The relevant materials were all written at a later time and in very different circumstances. It seems clear, however, from all the New Testament portraits of Jesus that he did not see his disciples as the beginning or the nucleus of an entirely new religion or a new Church, nor himself as the founder of such. Jesus lived and died as a pious Jew and, though he questioned the absoluteness of the law,[1] he attended the synagogue regularly and took part in the Temple festivals.[2] What we know of his preaching would indicate that his intention was to call his fellow Jews to conversion and reform. His disciples in that case would be the nucleus of such a reform.

It is in the context of this reform that he makes frequent use of the Jewish symbol of the "kingdom of God."[3] All three Synoptic Gospels sound this theme at the beginning of his public ministry. After John the Baptist was arrested, says Mark, "Jesus came into Galilee proclaiming the good news of God: 'The time has come; the kingdom of God is upon you; repent and believe the good news' " (Mark 1:14-15). Matthew's version is very similar, and Luke develops the theme further by connecting Jesus with the prophet Isaiah. On his visit to the synagogue in Nazareth Jesus read the Isaian prophecy about the one anointed and sent by the Spirit "to announce good news to the poor," and then says: "Today this Scripture has been fulfilled in your hearing" (Luke 4:16-21).

As Jesus' public ministry unfolds, many aspects of his activity find their theological meaning in the context of this fulfillment. The miracle tradition with its stories of Jesus healing the sick and curing the blind, feeding the hungry and forgiving sinners, are all instances of the good news of the inbreaking of God's kingdom. Many of Jesus' parables also focus on the kingdom, telling the people what it is like and what they must do to enter the kingdom.[4] Perhaps this also explains why Jesus restricted his preaching to his fellow Jews and why he instructed the Twelve whom he sent out to preach to go only "to the lost sheep of the house of Israel"

[1] See, for example, Mark 2:27-28: "The Sabbath was made for the sake of man and not man for the Sabbath: therefore the Son of Man is sovereign even over the Sabbath."

[2] See Luke's remark on the occasion of Jesus' visit to Nazareth, that he "went to the synagogue on the Sabbath day as he regularly did" (Luke 4:16).

[3] For the various interpretations and nuances of the kingdom metaphor at the time of Jesus, see Zachary Hayes, *Visions of a Future: A Study of Christian Eschatology* (Wilmington: Michael Glazier, 1989) 44-50.

[4] See, for example, Matt 13:44-52 and 25:31-46.

(Matt 10:6). In any case, as Zachary Hayes remarks, one of the most certain results of modern New Testament exegesis is the central importance of the kingdom in the preaching and ministry of Jesus.[5]

What is true of Jesus and his preaching is also true of his disciples even after his crucifixion and resurrection. They thought of themselves as faithful Jews, indeed as the true Jewish believers who had recognized and accepted the Messiah God had sent. They continued to go to the synagogue and "kept up their daily attendence at the Temple," with the added practice of sharing meals and "breaking bread in private houses" (Acts 2:46). Their preaching, like that of Jesus, was directed to their fellow Jews and continued to focus on the kingdom. Bultmann's remark that after the resurrection, "the proclaimer became the proclaimed," is only partially true. They continued to proclaim the kingdom as Jesus did, but in addition proclaimed him and his role in the realization of the kingdom. Peter's call for conversion at the Pentecost event, for example, mentions Jesus as the appointed Messiah through whom all that God had spoken through the mouths of the prophets would be fulfilled (Acts 2:14-36). Later when Philip visited the Samaritans he spoke of "the good news about the kingdom of God and the name of Jesus Christ" (Acts 8:12). Paul also connected the resurrection of Jesus with the kingdom: "We bring you the good news that what God promised to the fathers, this he has fulfilled to us their children by raising Jesus from the dead" (Acts 13:32-33).

The connection which Paul draws between resurrection and God's earlier promises helps explain the apparent conviction in the early Christian communities that the full realization of the kingdom and the second coming of Jesus was imminent. This imminent expectation was based on the belief that when the kingdom came the graves of the dead would be opened and they would be raised to life to inherit their share in the kingdom. For the disciples of Jesus, then, the experience of the risen Jesus was a sign that the end-time had arrived, and his resurrection was seen as the prelude to his imminent second and final coming. On this supposition their proclamation that God raised Jesus from the dead was not a departure from, but a continuation and confirmation of what Jesus himself had proclaimed, that "the kingdom of God was at hand." This

[5]*Op. cit.,* 44.

also explains the urgency of their message to their fellow Jews to repent and believe in the good news while there was still time.

There are many indications in the New Testament of this imminent, and in the event false, expectation. Writing to the Corinthians, Paul urges them to take heed lest they fall, "for the end of the ages has come upon us" (1 Cor 10:11). His advice to the married and to the unmarried is to remain in their present state, for "the appointed time has grown very short," and "the form of this world is passing away" (1 Cor 7:26-29; 31). He also exhorts the Christians at Rome to vigilance: "For salvation is nearer for us now than when we first believed; the night is far gone, the day is at hand" (Rom 13:11-12). In his First Letter to the Thessalonians Paul presumes that some of them will still be alive when the Lord comes: "For this we declare to you by the word of the Lord, that we who are alive, who are left until the coming of the Lord, shall not precede those who have fallen asleep" (1 Thess 4:15). Other books of the New Testament give evidence of the doubts raised by the delay of the Lord's coming. The Second Letter of Peter mentions those who are beginning to scoff and ask, "Where now is the promise of his coming?" The author reminds his readers that "with the Lord one day is like a thousand years, and a thousand years like one day," and he explains that "the Lord is not slow in fulfilling his promise," but is being patient and allowing time "for all to come to repentence" (2 Pet 3:3-9).

We find in the Gospels, too, indications that the end of the present age was expected within their own generation, and they even associate this expectation with Jesus himself. Jesus is reported to have told the people: "Truly, I say to you, there are some standing here who will not taste death before they have seen the kingdom of God already come in power" (Mark 9:1). When Jesus describes the signs that are to attend the last days when the Son of Man is to come in power, he warns the people: "Truly, I say to you, this generation will not pass away before all these things take place" (Mark 13:30). Matthew's Gospel expresses similar expectations. When Jesus sends the Twelve out to preach that "the kingdom of heaven is at hand," he describes the divisions and suffering their preaching will cause, but assures them: "You will not have gone through all the towns of Israel before the Son of Man comes" (Matt 10:23).

Whether Jesus himself shared these expectations, or whether

they originated in the early Christian communities as a result of their experience of the risen Jesus, it seems from the texts in Matthew and Mark as well as Paul that they were widespread among the early disciples. Though mistaken, they made sense as part of their interpretation of the experience of the risen Jesus as a sign of the end of the present age. But when their expectations were disappointed, they were forced to a different interpretation of the resurrection and a different understanding of themselves as the community of believers. For the nature of their community as a community of faith would be very different, depending upon whether they were awaiting the imminent return of the Lord or whether they had before them an indefinite and perhaps lengthy future. The disappointment of their expectations was one factor in bringing them to see themselves as something other than the remnant of true believers within the Jewish religion awaiting the final day of the Lord.

Another decisive factor in bringing them to a new self-understanding had to do with the membership of their community. All of the early members were Jews and they confined their preaching, as did Jesus, to their fellow Jews. The Acts of the Apostles describes the gradually widening horizon of their efforts from "Jerusalem, and all over Judaea and Samaria and away to the ends of the earth" (Acts 1:8). It tells in some detail the story of Peter's own conversion to this wider horizon (Acts 10:1-48). On a visit to the city of Joppa, Peter went up to the roof to say his prayers while his companions prepared the noonday meal. There he had a vision: a large sheet descended from heaven with all kinds of animals and reptiles and birds. A voice urged him to eat, but Peter protested: "No, Lord, no: I have never eaten anything profane or unclean." To this the voice rejoined, "It is not for you to call profane what God counts clean."

While Peter is puzzling over the meaning of his vision, a delegation arrives from Cornelius, a Roman centurian in Caesarea. Cornelius, too, has had a vision which instructed him to send to Joppa for Peter. Peter accompanies the messengers to Caesarea but mentions his misgivings about entering the house of Cornelius. "A Jew," he explains, "is forbidden by his religion to visit or associate with a man of another race." But Peter has received instructions on this point too: "God has shown me clearly that I must not call any man profane or unclean." Peter then puts the two and two of his visions together and arrives at what was for him a startling conclusion: "I now see how true it is that God has no favorites, but that in every nation anyone who fears him and does what is right is acceptable to him." It was not easy for Peter, a pious Jew, to have the Jewish dietary laws and the law against Gentile association thrown into question as he was brought to a new understanding of his discipleship.

As he was telling Cornelius and his household about the events of Jesus' crucifixion and resurrection, "the Holy Spirit came upon all who were listening to his message." The Jewish Christians who had accompanied Peter were "astonished that the gift of the Holy Spirit should have been poured out even on Gentiles." But Peter asks how anyone can withhold the water of baptism from the Gentiles "who have received the Holy Spirit just as we did ourselves." The story ends with Peter having Cornelius and his household "baptized in the name of Jesus Christ." When Peter returned to Jerusalem he encountered criticism for "visiting men who are uncircumcised and sitting at table with them." His explanation satisfied his critics who were as surprised as Peter "that to the Gentiles also God has granted repentence unto life."

Paul encountered the same kind of tension and criticism when his missionary work attracted Gentiles as well as Jews. In one incident at the synagogue at Antioch (Acts 13:42-47), Paul created such lively interest by his preaching on Jesus that he was invited back the following Sabbath. When he returned, "almost the whole city gathered to hear the word of God." But when the Jews saw the crowd, "they were filled with jealousy" and contradicted and reviled Paul. He insisted that he was following the command of the Lord: "I have appointed you to be a light for the Gentiles, that you may bring salvation to the uttermost parts of the earth." But there were those among the Jewish Christians who insisted on the basically Jewish nature of their community even if it were to include Gentiles. Some of them came from Judea to Antioch and began to teach their brethren: "Unless you are circumcised according to the custom of Moses, you cannot be saved" (Acts 15:1). This brought them into fierce conflict with Paul and Barnabas, and so heated was the dispute that the matter was taken to the apostles and elders in Jerusalem.

The apostles and elders gathered together in Jerusalem to discuss the matter and gave each side their say. Against those who were insisting that the Gentiles must keep the law of Moses, Peter repeats his discovery that God gave the Holy Spirit to the Gentiles just as he did to the Jews, making no distinction between them. Paul and Barnabas relate what signs and wonders God had worked among the Gentiles through them. At the end of the discussion James quotes the prophet Amos (9:11-12) who speaks of all the rest of mankind seeking the Lord and of the Gentiles whom God has claimed as his own. He concludes: "My judgment therefore is that we should impose no irksome restrictions on those of the Gentiles who are turning to God" (Acts 15:19). The judgment of James was accepted by the apostles and elders and the whole church, and was received with joy in Antioch.

The decision represents a watershed for the future development of the early Christian community. It meant that the community that had begun as exclusively Jewish and faithful to its Jewish heritage was now to be composed of Gentiles as well who were not bound by the Mosaic Law. This led eventually to the emergence of a new identity and new self-understanding. This development, along with the fact we have already considered, that Jesus did not return as expected and the community now faced the prospect of an open and indefinite future, brought about the transformation of the original more apocalyptic Jewish community into the Christian Church separate from Judaism. That this Church had its origins and foundation in Jesus is obvious enough. But given the historical factors involved in its emergence, which include the disappointments and surprises we considered, it is difficult historically to think of Jesus as explicitly "founding" the Church or "instituting" particular features of it. Rather he gave his disciples his Spirit who was to "guide" them and to "remind" them of him as their history unfolded.

That unfolding was to include the gradual development of particular structures required by their new situation, structures for which there was neither time nor need as they had understood their situation earlier. A comparison of two glimpses which we have of the early Christian communities might illustrate this development. Paul gives us a glimpse of the community in Corinth in his letters to them. At one point he mentions hearing that "when you assemble as a congregation there are divisions among you." As a result, he says, "It is impossible for you to eat the Lord's Supper, because each of you is in such a hurry to eat your own, and while one goes hungry another has too much to drink" (1 Cor 11:18; 20-21). After reminding them of the authentic tradition of the Lord's Supper and what it requires of them, Paul stresses in the next chapter the bond of unity that the Spirit ought to represent among them amidst the diversity of their many charisms, a bond that makes them a single body. It seems that the community was loosely organized "charismatically" around these various charisms or gifts of the Spirit.

Acts provides us with another glimpse which shows the beginnings of more structured organization to meet the needs of growing numbers. "During this period, when the disciples were growing in number, there was disagreement between those of them who spoke Greek and those who spoke Hebrew." The source of disagreement was the complaint by the Greek-speakers that "their widows were being overlooked in the daily distribution" at the table. (Acts 6:1). The Twelve called all the disciples together and proposed that the brethren choose "seven men of good repute, full of the Spirit and of wisdom" whom the Twelve would appoint to the duty of distributing the food equitably (Acts 6:3). The proposal proved acceptable to the whole community, so they elected their seven candidates and presented them to the apostles, "who prayed and laid their hands on them" (Acts 6:6).

Besides the need for a division of labor in the community, the text also speaks of appointment to a specific "duty" and describes the formal process of the laying on of hands by which those selected were appointed. All of this took place as "the disciples were growing in number," and it was natural that larger numbers required more structure and organization in the community. Comparing the earlier text of Paul with this text, there is evidence of a necessary development from the more "charismatic" community at Corinth, where Paul speaks of the different "spiritual gifts" and services distributed by the Spirit, to this more structured community of formal "offices" and duties decided by the community itself. The office of "deacon" had its origin as the practical solution to a practical problem.

The laying on of hands was a sign of the reception of the Holy Spirit, as another instance of its use makes clear. While the community of Antioch was at worship, they received word from the Holy Spirit to "set Barnabas and Saul apart for me, to do the work to which I have called them." After further fasting and prayer the community "laid their hands on them and let them go," and as they depart, the text comments that these two were "sent on their mission by the Holy Spirit" (Acts 13:2-4). The formal commissioning by the community is a sign of being sent by the Holy Spirit. The sign is also used to signify the reception of the Holy Spirit in the more general sense in which all the baptized receive the Holy Spirit. Such is the case when Peter and John visit converts in Samaria. They "had only been baptized in the name of the Lord Jesus," but the Holy Spirit "had not yet fallen on any of them." So Peter and John "laid their hands on them and they received the Holy Spirit" (Acts 8:14-17). There is an obvious parallel between the ritual of laying on hands in this instance, which later came to be called "confirmation," and its earlier use with the deacons, which later came to be called "ordination." Ordination is a further specification of the mission which all the confirmed receive from the Holy Spirit.

Another "structural" feature of the emerging Christian communities of which there is much evidence in the New Testament is a group within the community called the "elders." We have already mentioned the elders of the community in Jerusalem in connection with the controversy over the Mosaic Law. At the beginning, "The apostles and the elders gathered together to consider this matter" (Acts 15:6), and the decision is announced with the words, "It seemed good to the apostles and the elders, with the whole church . . ." (Acts 15:22). On their missionary journeys Paul and Barnabas would establish communities in the various cities they visited, and when they left to continue their missionary work, "They appointed elders for them in every church, and with prayer and fasting committed them to the Lord in whom they had put their faith" (Acts 14:23). Though mentioned frequently, the role of elders is not specified in any detail, but they would clearly constitute a kind of collegial leadership in the various local communities.

Another term that is used along with elder to designate this role is the Greek word *episkopos,* later to be translated "bishop," but which literally means one who oversees or one who is in charge. On one occasion Paul exhorts the "elders" of the church at Ephesus: "Keep watch over yourselves and over all the flock of which the Holy Spirit has made you overseers . . ." (Acts 20:28). In this passage the terms "elder" and "bishop" are used interchangeably. The same is true elsewhere, for example, in the Letter to Titus. He is told that he is to "appoint elders in every town," and when the letter goes on to describe the qualifications for being an elder, the other term "bishop" is used in its stead. When Paul sends greetings to the Philippians at the beginning of his letter, he addresses them "to all the saints in Christ Jesus who are at Philippi, with the bishops and deacons" (Phil 1:1). "Bishops" in the plural would refer to the same group known elsewhere as the elders.

This is significant because as the communities move into the second century a further development occurs in which the leadership of the community is invested not in a group of elders or bishops, but in a single bishop. This is attested to in the letters of Ignatius of Antioch to various Churches and soon becomes the uniform mode of government for all of the individual local Churches. The development was from a more collegial to a monarchical form of government. By the second century, of course, all of the apostles were gone, and they would have been the highest authority for all the Churches. But the leadership of the apostles, too, was more collegial than monarchical. Peter is very prominent in the early chapters of Acts as is Paul in the later chapters which describe the spread of the faith to the Gentiles. But in a matter of importance for all the Churches, such as was the case in the dispute about the Mosaic Law for the Gentile converts, the question was decided in collegial fashion and in accordance with what "seemed good to the apostles and the elders, with the whole church" (Acts 15:22).

This brief look at the emerging structures of the original Jewish communities as they evolved from their earlier situation of expectant anticipation of the Lord's return to more stable and permanent Christian Churches is further confirmation that the structures emerged in fidelity to the Spirit of the Lord rather than in accordance with an explicit design and intention received from Jesus himself. Whatever structures would enable them to live by his Spirit are in accordance with the intention of Jesus. His intention was that the community of his disciples continue to proclaim the kingdom of God as he had done: "As the Father sent me, so do I send you" (John 20:21), and he gave them the life and power of his Spirit to accomplish this. They were to do this until he returned, whatever the nature and duration of this "until." When the early disciples misinterpreted this "until" and were disappointed in their imminent expectation, they did not abandon their hope but recast it. They were still a community of hope when they became Church; they lived in hope for something beyond the Church. Their Church existed not for itself, as though this was the purpose of Jesus' life, death, and resurrection, but for the sake of the kingdom which he proclaimed and for which he gave his life.

Had Jesus returned as the early disciples expected, they would have shared immediately in his glory without having had to share in his Cross. The Church's "theology of glory" would not include the "theology of the Cross" as did that of Jesus. But a theology of glory becomes mere theory and hope becomes presumption without a practical theology of the Cross. The emergence of the Church, then, included the realization by the early disciples that the paschal mystery of the Cross as well as the resurrection is not only the central mystery of the life of Jesus, but also of his disciples.

The relationship of the Church to the kingdom makes clear the abiding and permanent significance of the Jewish religion for the Christian Church which emerged from it. The memory of Jesus, the "proclaimer" of the kingdom, prevents him from becoming merely the "founder" of a new Church. It prevents his actions with the bread and wine at the Last Supper by which he chose to be remembered, and which point to his real death on Calvary for the sake of the kingdom, from becoming merely the ahistorical and disembodied ritualism of a Church existing for itself and not for the kingdom. But when the Church performs these symbols "to proclaim the death of the Lord until he comes" (1 Cor 11:26), it proclaims his death and his resurrection as well within the larger history and the larger hopes of the kingdom still to come.

# 7

# Doing the Truth

When the theological meaning of the life, death, and resurrection of Jesus is seen in relationship to the kingdom, and the Church is understood as existing for the sake of the kingdom, many implications follow for Christian faith. Not least among them is the relationship between faith as theory and faith as practice, between holding things to be true and doing the truth. Karl Rahner once observed that one of the principle tasks facing contemporary theology is to transpose the theoretical doctrines of faith into practical imperatives so that "the theological as such will become a principle of action."[1] The "secular" reason for this task is contemporary historical consciousness and our new awareness of human responsibility for shaping and directing history. The theological reason is that what Jesus proclaimed in the past is still to come, so that theoretical statements of faith about his past entail hope in the future and action in the present for its realization.

It is God who created the world in the first place who must create the "new heaven and new earth" of the kingdom. But human beings have a role which Jesus described as *metanoia*, "conversion," and "faith": "The time has come; the kingdom of God is upon you; be converted and believe the Gospel" (Mark 1:15). Jesus' own faith reached its climax in his action on Calvary, and he described faith by saying that the disciple "must take up his cross and follow me" (Mark 8:34). Elsewhere in the Gospels Jesus is portrayed as pointing to his actions as the basis of faith in him:

[1] "Karl Rahner: An Interview," *America*, vol. 123, no. 13 (October 31, 1970), 358.

"My deeds done in my Father's name are my credentials," he said, adding: "I have set before you many good deeds, done by my Father's power; for which of these would you stone me?" (John 10:25, 32). Jesus' teaching became credible and persuasive not by the power of argument, but by the power of his actions. He promised this same power to his disciples when he told them after the resurrection: "You will receive power when the Holy Spirit comes upon you," and he described this as a power to "bear witness for me" (Acts 1:8).

The transliteration of the Greek word for witness is "martyr," and an event early in Acts shows that witness is given in deeds as well as words. It is the story of Stephen, who was one of the seven chosen to take care of the daily distribution of food to the widows. He was a man "full of grace and power" (Acts 6:8) who was arrested for blasphemy and brought before the High Priest and the Council. In his defense Stephen makes a lengthy speech about the patriarchs, Moses and the prophets, and ends with the story of Jesus being betrayed and put to death by his people. He tells them of a vision in which he "saw the glory of God, and Jesus standing at the right hand of God" (Acts 7:55). At this the Jews cried out against him, and taking him out of the city they stoned him to death. In his last words Stephen first commended himself to Jesus: "Lord, Jesus, receive my spirit." Then he implored forgiveness for his persecutors: "Lord, do not hold this sin against them" (Acts 7:59-60).

The parallels in Luke's account of Stephen's trial and death with those of Jesus are striking, and too close and too numerous to be accidental. Like Jesus, Stephen is accused of blasphemy and false witnesses are brought against him, and one of the things they accuse him of is saying that "Jesus of Nazareth will destroy this place." Like Jesus, Stephen prays for his persecutors and asks that his spirit be received. It is only in Luke's portrait of the death of Jesus that these last two details are recorded. What is Luke's theological point in making his accounts of the two deaths so similar?

Stephen's death was a new way of giving witness, indeed the way that was to become synonymous with the term "martyr." It added a further dimension to what it meant to be empowered by the Holy Spirit. The disciples were called upon to be witnesses not only of the resurrection of Jesus, but also of his death. The witness of Stephen was the actual process of "following" in his footsteps through death to resurrection. When Luke portrays Jesus explaining the Scriptures to the two disciples at Emmaus (24:27), and then to all the disciples (24:45), showing that the Christ had to suffer and *thus* enter into his glory, and saying that they had to be witnesses to all these things, he adds that the disciples were "slow of heart to believe." They were slow to believe not just in the resurrection, but also in the Cross, to believe that the Cross leads to resurrection, first in the life of Jesus, and then in the life of his disciple. Their faith had to be not merely a theoretical belief in the resurrection but the practical process of dying with him in order to rise with him.

It was only when Jesus himself did this truth that he overcame the slowness of the disciples to believe and to understand what he had told them. Peter is the focus of this theme in several Gospels. When Jesus spoke of the prospect of his own suffering, death, and resurrection, "Peter took him by the arm and began to rebuke him." Jesus' retort to Peter was sharp: "Away with you, Satan; you think as men think, not as God thinks" (Mark 8:32-33; also Matt 16:22-23). In John when Peter protested at Jesus' washing his feet, Jesus said: "You do not understand now what I am doing, but one day you will" (John 13:6-7). Finally, after the resurrection when Jesus hints at the death Peter is to die by telling him that you too "will stretch out your arms," he ends by repeating the invitation: "Follow me" (John 21:18-19). Peter finally came to understand and, like Stephen, was to follow and give witness in the ultimate sense of these terms.

It is from the perspective of what both John and the Synoptic Gospels call "following" that Paul develops his theology of Christian baptism. As the initiation rite into the Christian community, the meaning of baptism must be derived from the meaning and nature of the community. For Paul the Church is the community of those who are participating in the paschal mystery of the life, death, and resurrection of Jesus:

> Do you not know that all of us who have been baptized into Christ Jesus were baptized into his death? We were buried, therefore, with him by baptism into death, so that as Christ was raised from the dead by the glory of the Father, we too might walk in the newness of life. For if we have been united with him in a death like his, we shall certainly be united with him in a resurrection like his (Rom 6:3-5).

Baptism by total immersion into water is a graphic symbol of the reality it expresses, dying and rising with Jesus: "For in baptism you were buried with him, and in baptism also you were raised to life with him . . ." (Col 2:12). Entering into the water and emerging from it symbolize the passage through death to new life, becoming thereby part of "a new creation; behold, the old has passed away and the new has already begun" (2 Cor 5:17).

Paul bases his theology of baptism on the nature of the community into which one is initiated, and this in turn is based on the meaning of the life, death, and resurrection of Jesus. The paschal mystery, the central mystery of the life of Jesus, is also the central mystery of the life of the Church because it is his body, and this is the mystery symbolized in the rite of baptism. Baptism proclaims the death and resurrection of the Lord and the death and resurrection of the believer with him. But like the death of the Lord, the death of the believer takes place not in ritual but in real life to which the ritual points. It is there that one must bear witness to Jesus by the power of his Spirit until he comes again. By thus embodying his Spirit in its life, the community becomes the new Temple of the Lord's presence. They are "living stones" forming "a spiritual temple" (1 Pet 2:5), which is bonded together in Christ the "cornerstone" and "grows into a holy temple in the Lord" (Eph 2:20-21).

Understanding the community of the baptized as the living Temple of God's presence which replaces the Jewish Temple also means that the Temple sacrifices and the Temple priesthood have been replaced. The Letter to the Hebrews develops this new meaning of sacrifice and priesthood in the new covenant which Jesus has sealed, and it is only there that Jesus is called a "high priest." The title has a dissonant ring when applied to the Jesus portrayed in the four Gospels, for it is clear in their portraits that he was not a priest or high priest in the Jewish sense of these terms. There he is called "rabbi," "teacher," and "prophet," and these titles correspond to his life as itinerant preacher and reformer. But he is nowhere associated with the levitical priesthood of his time who were responsible for offering the Temple sacrifices. It is not surprising, then, that the title "priest" as a designation for Jesus is absent in all the other books of the New Testament.

Nor is it surprising that the author of Hebrews takes great pains to distinguish his use of the term in applying it to Jesus from how it would be understood in a Jewish sense. The priesthood of Jesus is not the levitical priesthood reserved to the descendants of Aaron, for he "belongs to a different tribe, no member of which has ever had anything to do with the altar" (Heb 7:13). His priesthood marks the beginning of a "new covenant" and means the abolition of the old covenant and the old priesthood (Heb 8:7-8). What distinguishes the new priesthood from the old is that "the blood of his sacrifice is his own blood, not the blood of goats and calves" (Heb 9:12). The power of his sacrifice derives from its being the offering of his own blood in self-sacrifice. Moreover, the offering of his blood took place not in the Temple, but "outside the city gate, to consecrate the people by his own blood" (Heb 13:12).

The difference between the levitical priesthood and the priesthood of Jesus is not that the latter replaces the old cult and ritual with a new one but that it replaces cultic and ritual sacrifice with real sacrifice. When applied to Jesus, then, the term "priest" has more to do with the tradition of the suffering servant in Isaiah and the prophet-martyrs than with the offering of cultic sacrifice by a cultic priest. The author of Hebrews immediately draws the implications of this for those who have been baptized into his death: "Let us then go to him outside the camp, bearing the stigma that he bore" (Heb 13:13). The offering of self in self-sacrifice is to be the essential meaning of priesthood and sacrifice in the Church which has replaced the Jewish Temple built of stone with a "living temple."

The only other use of the terms "priest" or "priesthood" in the New Testament is their application to the entire community which has been incorporated into the priesthood of Jesus through baptism. On this theme the First Letter of Peter exhorts his readers to "become a holy priesthood" (1 Pet 2:5), and describes their community of faith as "a chosen race, a royal priesthood, a holy nation, God's own people . . ." (1 Pet 2:9). The book of Revelation also applies the term to the whole community of the faithful. It says that he who freed us from our sins with his life's blood has "made of us a royal house to serve as the priests of his God and Father . . ." (Rev 1:5-6). The same use of the term appears later in a hymn:

> Thou art worthy to take the scroll and to break its seals, for thou wast slain and by thy blood didst purchase for God men of every tribe and

language, people and nation; thou hast made of them a royal house, to serve our God as priests; and they shall reign upon earth (Rev 5:9-10).

Finally, Revelation says that all the faithful "shall be priests of God and of Christ, and shall reign with him for a thousand years" (Rev 20:6).

In the New Testament, then, the term priest is applied in the first instance to Jesus in the new sense that the author of Hebrews elaborates, and then to the community of the baptized as having been constituted by Jesus into a new priesthood. It is not used in the New Testament of a particular office or ministry in the community. On the basis of Hebrew's new understanding of priesthood, which is derived from the nature of Jesus' death as self-sacrifice, and of Paul's understanding of baptism as being baptized into the death of Jesus, the priesthood of all the faithful can and should be understood as a participation in the priesthood of Jesus and from him acquire its meaning. It is not a cultic priesthood like the levitical priesthood of the Jewish Temple, but the real priesthood of taking up one's Cross and following him, of dying with him in order to rise with him. Its power is a participation in the power of his priesthood, which is the power of his love. It is the power conferred by the Spirit in baptism to bear witness to him by doing the truth that he did.

With the passage of time and the further development of structures and offices in the Church, the term priest came to be used in a different sense. It came to be associated with the Church's cultic and liturgical life and applied to the person who presided over the Church's liturgy. From the beginning, of course, when the early Christians gathered in their homes to break bread, someone would have led their celebration. It is not this role itself that is in question but how it was understood and named. It came to be called the role of priest, and so thorough was this development that for all practical purposes the term came to be understood exclusively in this new and cultic sense. In the middle ages priesthood came to be defined as a *deputatio ad cultum,* a responsibility for the Church's cultic activity, and its power was understood as a *potestas in corpus Eucharisticum,* a power exercised in the ritual celebration of the Eucharist. Insofar as the term "priest" has here acquired a very restricted and cultic sense, its meaning is really closer to that of the levitical priesthood of the Old Testament than to the New Testament priesthood of Jesus.

However understandable and legitimate this development might be from a sociological point of view given the changes and developments in the Church's social structure, from a theological point of view the New Testament meaning of priesthood is not only the original but also the essential and fundamental meaning of Christian priesthood. For the priesthood of Jesus is based not on his action at the Last Supper, but on his action on Calvary to which the Last Supper points. The ongoing celebration of the Lord's Supper in the Church retains this same relationship to his death on Calvary and to the death of all those who have been baptized into his death. The mystery of the Eucharist is the paschal mystery of the death and resurrection of Jesus, and of all those who have been empowered by the Spirit to participate in this mystery. The essential power of Christian priesthood is this real participation, not in the first instance a juridical or cultic power, and this real participation is the essential and fundamental way that one shares in the priesthood of Jesus.

The primary sacrament of Christian priesthood, then, is baptism, including the second part of this initiation rite which was later separated off and became the sacrament of confirmation. For it is in baptism, as Paul explains, that one is baptized into the paschal mystery of Jesus' death and resurrection, and thereby into his priesthood in its specifically Christian sense. One particular way of living out the Christian priesthood of baptism is through the ministry conferred by the sacrament of orders. But all the ministries in the Church and all the variety of gifts and powers of the Spirit are so many different ways of living out this same priesthood in which all the members of the Church share. The priesthood of orders cannot be distinguished from the others as a "ministerial priesthood," for all the particular ways of exercising priesthood are forms of ministry or service. Like the priesthood of Jesus whose self-sacrifice was for the sake of the kingdom, all these different ministries participate in the mission of the Church to proclaim and to share in his death for the sake of the kingdom until he comes.

Theologically it would be a reversal of priorities, putting the Church before the kingdom, and historically a reversal of the way things actually developed in the Church, to think of the priesthood of orders as the primary Christian priesthood and of the baptismal priesthood of all the faithful as a lesser participation in the priesthood of orders which ordained priests have in a fuller way. It is rather the opposite which is the case. The priesthood of orders is but one way of participating in and living out the priesthood of baptism which everyone shares equally. For the paradigm and prime analogate of Christian priesthood is the priesthood which Jesus enacted and "instituted" on Calvary by offering "his own blood," as Hebrews says. His call to share this priesthood is given indiscriminately to all his disciples: "Anyone who wishes to be a follower of mine . . . must take up his cross and follow me" (Mark 8:34). This is the primary and essential call to Christian priesthood. It does not distinguish between "Jew or Greek, slave or free, male or female" (Gal 3:28), nor, we could add, between lay and cleric. Whoever follows more closely is the one who participates more fully in the priesthood of Jesus.

When these priorities are reversed and orders replaces baptism as the primary sacrament of Christian priesthood, the priesthood of all the faithful is seen as a lesser participation in what priests or bishops have more fully. The "non-priests" can, for example, be lectors or help to distribute communion, but they do not have the "power" to do the real thing. Such an understanding sacralizes and trivializes the priesthood of Jesus, for it reduces it to a matter of cultic and ritual activity like the levitical priesthood and removes it from the realm of history and real life where Jesus exercised his priesthood by actually giving his life for the kingdom. He who proclaimed the kingdom and inaugurated a new historical age is reduced to the founder of a new religious cult to replace the Temple cult. But the power of Jesus' priesthood is not primarily a cultic power. It is rather the power of his love and the power of his Cross. This is the power he gave to his disciples when he breathed his Spirit upon them and sent them, as he was sent, to bear witness to him "to the ends of the earth."

In his version of the sending of the Spirit John makes explicit an important aspect of this power of the Spirit. On the first Easter night when Jesus appeared to the disciples he breathed on them and said: "Receive the Holy Spirit. If you forgive the sins of any, they are forgiven; if you retain the sins of any, they are retained" (John 20:22-23). Jesus' own power to forgive sins is a recurrent theme in the gospel portraits of his ministry. It is an aspect of his work of reconciliation in offering table fellowship to all, including

the publicans and sinners. As part of his priestly power to recon-
cile human beings to God and to one another, it is not limited
to the liturgical exercise of this power by ordained priests in what
developed into the sacrament of penance, but is exercised wherever and whenever divisions among human beings are healed and
the walls of hatred and prejudice are broken down. This task of
forgiveness and reconciliation is shared in different ways by all the
members of the Church as part of their baptismal priesthood. It
is when such real reconciliation is taking place among humankind
outside of Church that the Church's sacrament of reconciliation
becomes a real sign and symbol of the presence and power of the
Spirit in the ongoing history of Jesus today.

It is also true, of course, that not all were called to be apostles
at the time of Jesus, nor were all appointed elders or bishops in
the Apostolic Church. The author of Hebrews tells his readers to
"obey your leaders" (Heb 13:17). The early Church and the early
Churches had a differentiated structure from the beginning, and
these structures were to evolve into a variety of authorities and
offices as the Church gradually became more institutionalized.
Among them the priesthood of orders developed into a particular
office and ministry of leadership in the Church. Such developments
were understandable and legitimate given the various sociological
factors at work in the Church's history. To affirm the priority of
the priesthood of baptism is not to question the legitimacy of these
developments. It is rather to see every kind of office or authority
in the Church as rooted in baptism, for only the baptized can assume such an office or position of authority. However important
for the life of the Church such offices and structures might be, what
all Christians have in common is more important and more central to Christian faith than what differentiates them: "One Lord,
one faith, one baptism" (Eph 4:5), and through this baptism one
Spirit who is given to all.

To affirm the priority of the priesthood of baptism is to affirm
the priority of Scripture as the ultimate norm for the life and practice of the Church. This is not to subscribe to the principle of
"Scripture alone," nor to think that the earliest form which the
life and practice of the Church took is the necessary form for all
subsequent ages and in all conceivable situations. For the Church
existed in a changing history at its beginnings and still does today.
Developments did in fact take place in the life and practice of the

Church during and after apostolic times, and had to take place given changing circumstances both inside and outside the Church in the world in which it existed. For the same reason similar changes are also possible today. The priority of Scripture means rather that these further developments are always derivative and secondary to what remains the abiding norm of the church's faith and practice. This must be so because it is through Scripture that the Church is tied to Jesus of Nazareth whose historical life and death is the beginning of the Church's history not only in the sense of the first moment, but also in the sense of its abiding principle and source.

Hence the importance of seeing in the scriptural witness to Jesus that the proclamation and inauguration of the kingdom was the central focus of his preaching and ministry. However inevitable was the origin of the Church given the actual outcome of the preaching of Jesus and of his first disciples, the Church always remains a function of the kingdom. It does not exist for itself, as though it had been the original concern and intention of Jesus, but for the sake of the kingdom. It exists for the purpose of continuing his call to conversion and faith, not faith in the Church, but faith in Jesus and hope in the coming of the kingdom of his Father. The Church does this insofar as it remains the living embodiment of the truth for which he lived and died by doing this same truth in its own life.

Hence also the importance of seeing the words and actions of Jesus with the bread and wine at the Last Supper as real symbols of his historical action on Calvary. When they are seen as having their meaning and reality in what he did at the supper rather than in what he did the following day, faith in the Eucharist is understood as a separate mystery of Christian faith. Then the Eucharist becomes *a* mystery rather than *the* mystery of Christian faith, the mystery in which the whole of Christian faith is contained and expressed because the symbols contain and express the paschal mystery of the life, death, and resurrection of Jesus. This separation has its parallel in the interpretation of Christian priesthood. It is understood primarily as a separate role and function in the Church, and its "power" as a separate and cultic power. This distorts the fundamental meaning of Christian priesthood which is the actual participation by all the faithful through baptism and the power of the Spirit in the paschal mystery of the life, death, and resurrection of Jesus.

When the priesthood of Jesus in this way loses its roots in his historical action on Calvary, that is, in his death for the sake of the kingdom, so too does participation in his priesthood lose its roots in historical action for the sake of the kingdom in the present. It becomes a priesthood for the sake of the Church rather than a priesthood for the sake of the kingdom. The liturgical proclamation and remembrance of his death and the cultic representation of his sacrifice on the cross become dissociated from the ongoing history of his death and his Cross in the living and dying of his disciples today. Liturgy is separated from life and the sanctuary from the world, and they assume a sacral life of their own. Validity replaces reality as the measure of the Church's liturgy. But if the focus of Jesus' life and ministry is the kingdom of his Father, and if the focus of the Last Supper symbols is his death for the sake of this kingdom, then his past history becomes part of his still unfinished history in the present as it moves towards its final consummation in his future coming.

# 8

# Through a Glass Darkly

When the history of Jesus is seen as part of the larger history of God's presence and activity in the world, and the life of Jesus is seen as the beginning of a new age in this history, an age that is still unfolding and will continue to unfold until the end of time through his Spirit at work in the disciples who heed his call to "follow" him, two aspects of faith in Jesus come especially to the fore. Faith in the first instance is a matter of practice, the actual process of following him and of being involved in his ongoing history. Second, the theoretical expression of this faith which necessarily follows upon practice will be Trinitarian. The Christological moment which reflects upon the theology of Jesus will be seen in the broader context of the theology of the Father and the theology of the Spirit. All three of these moments together constitute the single content of Christian faith, the content that was revealed in the paschal mystery and comes to expression in the Last Supper symbols as *the* mystery of Christian faith.

The Trinitarian mystery revealed in Jesus is not merely the mystery of God but the mystery of God and the world. Christian faith is not about God's nature but God's freedom, not about *what* God necessarily is but about *who* God has freely chosen to be in relation to us and who we are in relation to God as a result. Christian faith is about the coming to be of this mutual relationship in time. It is of this relationship that Christian Scripture speaks. That is why it is said to announce "news," indeed, "good news." The Scriptures speak not of an eternal and necessary state of affairs but of contingent events which happened and are to happen in history.

That is why history as the locus of these events is their central focus, not only past history, but the present and future as well, for their narrative is unfinished. It is in history that the relationship happened and was revealed, and in history that it is still happening and is still to be revealed.

It is because Christian faith is about this relationship that is still in the making that Christian faith is essentially a "following" and a "doing." It does not offer a comfortable theory about how things will turn out but a challenging hope about how things can turn out, challenging because hope includes human action for its realization. Although the initiative for God's relationship to the world lies in God's freedom, and it is God's power that will bring about its consummation, it cannot happen without human freedom as well. The power of God as revealed in Jesus is the power of love; hence it presents human beings with an offer and a call, not with an accomplished fact. As a relationship of love, God's relationship to the world is a personal relationship that requires two freedoms and two "yes's," that of the offer and that of the response. Human beings cannot save themselves but they cannot be saved without themselves. Jesus proclaimed the coming of the kingdom, the reign of God's love, but wept over Jerusalem because she did not recognize the time of her visitation.

The abiding significance of the history of Jesus is that he revealed the truth of God's offer to the world, the truth that God had created it with the potentiality to be his kingdom, and in his life, death, and resurrection he actualized this potentiality and realized this truth through his free acceptance and response. By loving "unto the end," as John says, he was in his life and person the beginning of the triumph of God's love over the power of sin, evil, and death. This is the triumph which Scripture calls the kingdom or the reign of God's love. Hence with him came the "firstfruits" of the power of God's love and he is the "firstborn of many brothers and sisters." In the same vein the author of Hebrews calls him the "pioneer" of our faith, for he has opened and shown the way by actually going this way himself. By thus becoming the way for others, he is not only the beginning of this new life, but also its principle and source for those who follow.

Their path toward the kingdom is always the same path that he followed through his life, death, and resurrection, and the intrinsic relationship of these three moments shows that the alternative between the kingdom of God "here and now" and the kingdom of God "hereafter" is a false alternative. The relationship between the kingdom here and the kingdom hereafter is the relationship between his Cross and his resurrection. The culmination of his earthly life was the "hereafter" of the resurrection, but it was the culmination precisely of the "here and now" of all the moments he lived in life and in death. His risen life was not a replacement or an alternative to his earthly life but its fruit and culmination. His life and death in time were the passage into the new life of the resurrection. The passage to the kingdom always follows this path because it is only the power of love that can bring it about, both in its beginnings here and in its culmination hereafter. Like the risen existence of Jesus, these beginnings will not be replaced by the "new earth" but will be transformed and completed.[1]

The life, death, and resurrection of Jesus show that the alternative between God's role and the human role in bringing about the kingdom is an equally false alternative. The history of these two freedoms must include God's free initiative and a free human response, God's love and human love. The power of God's love is not an alternative to human love, but creates the possibility of human love. Nor is there any alternative between an "individual" and a "social" interpretation of the kingdom. For as Matthew's parable of the kingdom and the last day shows, the participation by individuals in the kingdom is dependent on their social relationships wherein their response to God is uttered and lived (Matt 25:31-46). Nor does this parable about feeding, clothing, and helping those in need make any distinction between "spiritual" and "material" help or between "evangelization" and "pre-evangelization." The acts he describes are acts of compassion and love, and this is the power of which the evangelists speak and through which the kingdom comes.

When the history of Jesus is faithfully remembered for the sake of its continuation today, theoretical beliefs about his past become practical principles of action in the present. Believing "in" Jesus includes believing "with" him, and faith *in* Jesus includes associa-

---

[1]See Karl Rahner's reflections on the "new earth" in "The Theological Problems Entailed in the Idea of the 'New Earth,' " *Theological Investigations* 10 (New York and London, 1973), 260–72, and "Immanent and Transcendent Consummation of the World," *op. cit.*, 273–89.

tion with and participation in the faith *of* Jesus. Such association is possible because he breathed upon his disciples the Spirit who had descended upon him and he sent them as he was sent by the Father. He gave them the same Spirit who was the source of his life and power. Because the work of Jesus is incomplete without the work of the Spirit, faith in Jesus must include faith in the presence and activity of the Spirit today.

Christian tradition elaborated the doctrine of the Trinity in order to be able to speak of the relationship between God and the world in a way that did justice both to the reality of God and the reality of the world. Because of the incarnation of God's son, this relationship is one of unity in difference: God and the world are never identical, but neither are they ever separate. This unity in difference between God and the world requires that God's own being be one of unity in difference. If it is really God's own self who is related to the world through the Son and the Spirit, the Son and the Spirit must belong to God's own reality and not merely be "modes" of God's appearance to us. The reality of God's Trinitarian relationship to us requires that God's own being be Trinitarian.

God's Trinitarian relationship to the world also tells us what the world is like if it is capable of this relationship. It tells us that the utterly transcendent and sovereign God has created the world in such a way that it has the potentiality of sharing God's own life in knowledge and love, a potentiality beyond its own inherent powers. Indeed, it is a potentiality beyond any created power and belongs properly only to God. In freely creating the world in this way, then, the same God who is transcendent to the world must also be immanent within the world as its own intrinsic potentiality and power to become more than itself, to actually share God's life. If, as the prologue to John's Gospel says, "the Word became flesh," God's immanence must be the intrinsic source of the potentiality for such becoming within flesh. If God became flesh, flesh cannot be totally alien to God's becoming, and yet its affinity for such becoming must be due to God. The God who created it for this purpose must be immanent within creation as well as transcendent to it.

Likewise, if the same prologue says that all who receive the Word and give him their allegiance "become children of God" and "the offspring of God himself" (John 1:12-13), the God who created them must also be the immanent source within them of the potentiality for such a relationship to God. If God created the world to respond in love to God's love and thus to share God's own life, then God's own Spirit, who is love and the bond of union within God's own being, must also be the empowering source of this response of love within the world. Paul speaks of the Spirit as such an immanent principle within creation:

> For all who are moved by the Spirit of God are sons of God. The Spirit you have received . . . makes us sons, enabling us to cry "Abba! Father!" In that cry the Spirit of God joins with our spirit in testifying that we are God's children (Rom 8:14-16).

Preeminently, then, in the incarnate life of the Logos, and in the life of grace lived by all God's children, the Spirit is the immanent principle and potentiality within created reality who empowers and enables it to share God's life.

It is in the context of the presence of God's Spirit within all of creation and all of history as the offer and potentiality for grace that the historical moment of Jesus has its importance for Christian faith. In his free response to this offer the fullest and highest potential of human flesh became actual in history. In him the eternal relationship of the Son to the Father became flesh because he freely lived a human life of sonship throughout his life and "unto the end" in his death. This event in time and history reveals how Christian faith sees the relationship between transcendence and history. Transcendence is not a leap out of the world and history to God, for God in the Spirit is within the world and in the Son became flesh in history. Transcendence is rather the potentiality within the world and history to move by the power of the Spirit toward God and the kingdom, a potentiality which becomes actual in human freedom and historical action.

Because the one Spirit of God is present and active in history today as it was in the history of Jesus, they are parts of a single history of which the Spirit is the bond. The history of the Christian community today can be the continuation of the history of which Jesus was the beginning and source because the same Spirit who animated its beginnings is at work as it unfolds in the present. The Spirit is not only the principle of unity in Paul's image of the single Body of Christ but also the principle of association with him in his ongoing history, binding together all successive ages of his single history. The Spirit is not a principle of sameness in

this history, but of adaptation and change as the community encounters different cultural situations. For it is not fidelity to the
same "letter" but fidelity to the same Spirit which gives this history its unity and cohesion.

But the Spirit is the principle of unity not only within the history of the Christian community but also of this history with the
larger history beyond its boundaries. If God's immanence within
the world in the Spirit is given with creation and came not as a
subsequent afterthought, all of created history is bound together
in God's Spirit as a single history. The Spirit who descended upon
Jesus at his baptism came not as a stranger to God's creation but
had been its innermost dynamism from the beginning.[2] The unique
historical moment of Jesus is united through the Spirit with every
historical moment in every time and culture. The universal presence of the same Spirit who is the Spirit of Jesus is what prevents
his particular history from becoming a particularism of exclusivist
claims. What Christians have in common with all men and women
of all times and cultures is more central to their human and Christian identity than what distinguishes them. Their faith in Jesus does
not separate them from those outside the church but unites them.

The presence of God's Spirit throughout all of creation means
that this presence is universal not only in the sense of all people
in all times and cultures but also in the further sense of all the
dimensions of this creation. The presence of the Spirit is not limited to a special compartment of life such as the "religious" or
"spiritual" realm. The material world was not created merely to
be the external stage upon which a spiritual drama was played out.
Rather all dimensions of life are involved in the drama and share
in the purpose of God's creation. Just as the presence of the Spirit
overcomes any gnostic dualism between God and the world and
sees the two as positively interrelated, so too does it overcome any
dualism within this creation. God can be found "in all things" because all things, whether they belong to the sacred or secular or
the spiritual or material realm, can and should embody the Spirit
of God who is the Spirit of love.

[2]To express the universal presence of God's offer of grace intrinsic to creation Karl Rahner called it a "supernatural existential." See "Concerning the
Relationship between Nature and Grace," *Theological Investigations* 1 (Baltimore
and London, 1961), 297–317, especially 310–17.

All things, of course, including religious and spiritual things, can be the embodiment of the opposite of God's Spirit, the opposite of love which is sin. This spirit too, as the story of the Fall in Genesis indicates, has been present almost from the beginning. It too is a potentiality which has been actualized and embodied in history, and in its transmission through history from generation to generation has been called "original sin." But it is Christian faith that grace is more original than original sin, and it is Christian hope that it is also more final. This faith and hope see in the coming of Jesus the beginning of the triumph of the Spirit of love over the spirit of sin, and await in his second coming its final triumph. Jesus called this triumph the kingdom of his Father, the reign of God over all the powers of evil, even the power of death. The final triumph of the Father and his reign is the third element in the Church's Trinitarian faith in Jesus.

The first two elements, each in its own distinct way, speak of God's presence and immanence in the world. Jesus is the incarnation and embodiment of God's life in history, the fullest actualization of a possibility which is given within creation because God's Spirit has been present from the very beginning of creation as the universal call and innermost potentiality of created reality to share this life. But however much God freely becomes present in the world and history, and however much God created the world to be the body wherein God's own Spirit was to dwell, God is no less transcendent to the world. God and the world are never separate, but neither are they ever identical in any form of pantheism. This element of the transcendence of God is expressed in the third name which God bears. God is the transcendent source and creator from whose sovereign freedom all things have come, and God is the final, transcendent goal toward whom they are moving through God's freedom and theirs.

Christian tradition also speaks of our human relationship to this Trinitarian God by three different names: faith, hope, and love. If faith describes the process of following and association with Jesus in his ongoing history in time, love describes the content of the life which lives by the Spirit of Jesus and the Spirit of God, and hope best describes the movement through time with Jesus and in his Spirit toward the kingdom of his Father. For one hopes for something which one does not yet possess, and the possession of which lies not in one's own power, but in the power of another.

Jesus faced the powerlessness of death in hope in his Father, in hope that loving "unto the end" was a beginning and the seed of new life. Scripture speaks of the fulfillment of his hope by saying that "God raised him from the dead" (Acts 3:15). The hope of all Christians, like the hope of Jesus, is always in a power that lies beyond their own.

Paul speaks of the transcendence of God in an image that describes this hope well. At the end of his description of love as the preeminent gift of the Spirit and the necessary way of Christian life, he says that one day "we shall see face to face." But here and now while still on the way "we see only through a glass darkly" (1 Cor 13:12). Other translations render the last phrase "puzzling" or "dim reflections in a mirror." To a contemporary of Paul's the meaning of the metaphor would have been immediately obvious. For at the time mirrors were made not of glass, but of polished metal, casting a dark image of the object reflected. Seeing God, Paul's metaphor says, is like seeing something in a mirror. One sees not the reality itself, but its dark, imperfect image or reflection cast by the mirror. But the imperfect image grounds the hope of one day seeing the reality itself "face to face."

For Paul, of course, the human face of Jesus was the image and "glass" par excellence: "He is the image of the invisible God" (Col 1:15). His human life and death were the incarnation and revelation of God's life present and imaged in flesh. But in a lesser way all human living and dying and all of created reality, when it lives by and embodies the Spirit that animated Jesus and is part of his history and not the history of sin, can provide reflections and glimpses of the God who is the source of this Spirit in creation. Indeed, all history in the most secular meaning of the term is the history of salvation and the coming of God's kingdom when, like the history of Jesus, it embodies in space and time that way of life which is the life of God, namely, the life of love. When seen from the perspective of the world and its history, the second "coming" of Jesus is the movement of history in hope by the dynamism of his Spirit toward its final consummation in the kingdom of the Father.

Paul's metaphor of the mirror can be expressed in the language of the later tradition by saying that all our knowledge of God is by analogy with created realities. This traditional understanding of the analogy of being was based on God's transcendence as the creator and source of all things which reflect the being of their maker. But if God is also immanent within the world bringing about a "new creation" begun by Jesus and carried on in his Spirit, this immanence grounds a new and deeper analogy of being. It is an analogy based on the new being and new life bestowed by the Spirit. If this Spirit is truly God's Spirit, this new being and life is truly a participation in God's own being and life. Those who live this life are "not born of any human stock," John says, but are "the offspring of God himself" (John 1:13). Because it is an analogy of being, it precludes any kind of univocal identification of all things with God as in pantheism. The analogy does not lessen God's transcendence of the world. But because God is also immanent, the analogy precludes the total disparity of a God who is remote and distant from the world as in deism. The analogy of this new being and new life, the analogy of grace, says rather that God and the world are never identical, but neither are they ever separate.

The analogy of being based on God's new creation is also the source of knowledge of God for those who share in this new creation through faith. But if faith is primarily the actual practice and process of association with Jesus, this knowledge is not in the first instance a theoretical knowledge of God. It is rather an experiential knowledge derived from actually sharing God's life in its created analogues. It is not through concepts that are analogous to God's being that one knows God, but through living a life that is analogous to God's life. Human love is the created analogue of divine love. This "created grace" is the "glass" in which "uncreated grace" is experienced. Paul uses the sense of sight when he speaks of seeing God "through a glass darkly," but including the other senses as well brings out the experiential nature of this knowing. One can also speak with the psalmist of "tasting" the goodness of the Lord and of touching and being touched by God's goodness as experienced in created analogues. Faith brings new knowledge because it first brings new life wherein God is known experientially by sharing his life.

In such knowledge God is not known as an object, but, as John's reflections on knowing God through loving one's neighbor suggest (1 John 4:7-9), in this lived relationship to one's neighbor God is known by connaturality with divine life. It is knowledge in the sense of a personal union with God, not in the sense of a theory about God. Such implicit or unthematic knowledge of God in the midst of life can and must be objectified and made explicit, as Paul does when he speaks of one day knowing God "face to face." But knowledge of God is not limited to the realm of the explicitly religious or the realm of spirituality. If God's Spirit is immanent in all of created reality, God can be encountered in the created analogues of God's life throughout the whole materiality of his creation. Indeed, explicit religious knowledge of God becomes real knowledge, and not merely ideas about God, only when it is rooted in experience and lived faith. One discovers what the paschal mystery of the life of Jesus means by sharing in it in the secular as well as the sacred dimensions of life.

Paul's dialectic of "then" and "now," of "face to face" and "through a glass darkly," emphasizes the role of hope in our knowledge of God and the kingdom. "For we have been saved," he says elsewhere, "though only in hope" (Rom 8:24). Salvation and God's kingdom are experienced "only in hope," only in their created analogues which point to their full realization in a future that is yet to come. Hence he calls our present knowledge of God "partial" and he looks forward in hope to knowing one day "even as I am known" (1 Cor 13:12). However much God has made the world and its history his own history through the presence of the Spirit and by becoming incarnate in flesh, God remains ever the transcendent and hidden God: "For my thoughts are not your thoughts, and your ways are not my ways," said Isaiah, but his conclusion is one of hope that the Lord's word "shall prevail" and not return "fruitless" (Isa 55:8, 11).

When the transcendence of God and the kingdom are forgotten, hope is replaced by its caricature which the tradition calls presumption. Presumption presumes that what is hoped for is a present possession by identifying some relative, penultimate reality with the absolute and the ultimate itself. Presumption characterizes the religion of a fanatic whose zeal is identified with God's zeal and pursued in God's name, or a totalitarian religion which identifies its law with divine law, its authority with divine authority, its teaching with divine truth. Presumption also has its secular versions which absolutize some finite reality such as progress, reason, science, or a political or economic system, and think that therein lie the resources for human beings to create their own kingdom. In both cases some finite reality, be it religious or secular, is absolutized into an idol. In its own way the opposite of presumption, despair, is also the denial of a transcendent God. Human reality has no ultimate purpose or meaning and can offer no hope in the future. Paul's metaphor places hope between presumption and despair and sees in the "glass" of penultimate realities in the present the foretaste and promise of God's transcendent and absolute future.

The Church's ancient liturgical prayers, which were addressed to the Father through the Son and in the Holy Spirit, and the earliest form of the doxology, "Glory be to the Father, through the Son, and in the Holy Spirit," express the Trinitarian structure of the Church's faith. It was through the historical reality of the Son, with whom they were united in the Spirit, that the community approached and addressed the transcendent God of its faith and hope. Its Trinitarian faith and hope embraced both God and the world, for a purely otherworldly, ahistorical God does not exist. A "pure divine nature" that would exist in separation from a "pure human nature" can be conceived as an abstract possibility, but has been outstripped in God's sovereign freedom by the events of history which have brought them into relationship. Insofar as the Church exists to participate in the ongoing history of these events until the relationship between God and the world reaches its final stage in the kingdom, the world and history are more central and fundamental to Christian faith and hope than is the Church itself.

From this perspective the words and actions of Jesus with the bread and wine at the Last Supper constitute a "short formula" of Christian faith, recapitulating in summary form the heart of this faith. The symbols express not *a* mystery, but *the* mystery of Christian faith, for they express the paschal mystery of the life, death, and resurrection of Jesus through whom the kingdom was inaugurated. When his historical action in the past is seen in relation to the work of the Spirit today, the symbols become a principle of action in the present. In this action of the Church for the sake of the kingdom, the symbols also express the paschal mystery of the life of the Church. They embody not only the mystery of Christian faith, but the mystery of Christian love and Christian hope as well. It is in this hope that the Church continues to proclaim and share his death until he comes, when in the kingdom God will be known face to face.